D0045184

FROM TEXT TO SERMON
Responsible use of the New Testament in Preaching

From Text to Sermon

Responsible use of the New Testament in Preaching

By

Ernest Best

JOHN KNOX PRESS
ATLANTA

Library of Congress Cataloging in Publication Data

Best, Ernest.
    From text to sermon.

    Includes bibliographical references.
    1. Preaching.   2. Bible. N.T.—Hermeneutics.
3. Bible. N.T.—Theology.   I. Title.
BV4211.2.B46   251   77–79584
ISBN 0–8042–0245–1

© copyright 1978 John Knox Press
Printed in the U.S.A.
John Knox Press
Atlanta, Georgia

contents

FROM TEXT TO SERMON
Responsible use of the New Testament in Preaching

întroõuctíon

This is not a book about the theology of preaching or about its place
in the structure of worship. It does not discuss either the preacher as
herald of the gospel or his authority to proclaim God's Word. Least
of all is it concerned to talk about the way the material ought to be
presented, the nuts and bolts of sermon construction (an introduction,
three points, and a conclusion!), or the language in which the thought
should be clothed (avoid words derived from Latin and Germanically
turned phrases!). It does not set out to provide sermon outlines; it may
even lead to the destruction of some that already exist. Its purpose is
to see how we get from Scripture to God's message today, how the
Word which was once embodied in the words of Scripture may be
embodied in the words of the preacher, how the Jesus who spoke to
the readers of Paul and John through their words may speak to us
now. It is assumed that sermons will continue to be preached though
it is recognized that other methods of communication will be increas-
ingly brought into use. Most of the illustrations are drawn from the
New Testament, because the writer by the very nature of his occupa-
tion has to work with this every day, but almost all of what is said
about the New Testament could be said of the Old Testament, with
a minimum of necessary changes. The book is designed primarily for
preachers but it is hoped that it will also be of use to those who use
Scripture for meditation and enlightenment, whether to learn more of
God, to make up their minds on the right course of action in some
difficult situation, or to be able to express themselves adequately and
relevantly about their faith in a discussion group.

Scripture is not approached here for academic purposes but it is assumed that whatever academic knowledge the reader has will be brought to the task of interpretation (the more he has the better, for God gave us our minds to use). We do not come to Scripture to satisfy intellectual curiosity but because we believe that in it we find the focal point for our understanding of our faith.

Prior to the rise of the historical-critical method in the nineteenth century many books were written on the science of hermeneutics and in them advice was given on the rules for interpreting Scripture. Within the last three decades the discussion of hermeneutics has been revived but in a totally different direction. It has become an approach to theology, a way of systematizing theology, rather than a way of interpreting Scripture. The beginnings of this modern discussion were interesting and encouraging, but it has now run to seed and is of little help to those who are engaged in the day-to-day task of expounding Scripture. What is written here is written in the light both of the earlier part of the present discussion of hermeneutics and of the changed views we have of Scripture through the historical-critical method. What then should happen when someone takes a passage of Scripture and tries to understand it, not as an intellectual problem, but as a guide to life and thought? How can the Word which has already been confined within words, the words of Scripture, be set free so that it is confined again within our words? How can a man interpret the Scriptures in such a way that they themselves are interpreted and at the same time they interpret the interpreter and his life? We want to interpret Scripture so that we come to an understanding of God and ourselves. We want to unleash the Word that is in Scripture so that it becomes God's word to us today.

The first chapter begins with the New Testament and its nature, the second with the world in which we live and the differences between it and the world of the New Testament, the third treats some of the ways in which they are brought together and in the fourth some conclusions are drawn. The illustrations from sermons which are used have all been drawn from those who have been recognized as among the great preachers of the past; sometimes even they have failed! For obvious reasons, examples from living preachers have not been used.

The book was originally a set of lectures delivered in varying forms to the University of St. Andrews Summer School of Theology (1975), to the American Institute of Theology at St. Andrews (1975), to a refresher school of the Baptist Union of Scotland (1975), in the Presbyterian College, Belfast (1976), and to my own students. The criticisms of those who heard it have all been noted even if they have not always been accepted. I am also grateful to my own minister, the Reverend D.S.M. Hamilton, who not only read the manuscript but, more importantly, has continually inspired me with his preaching and proved for me that the ideas I have attempted to outline can indeed be carried into effect. Finally, my thanks are due to my secretary, Mrs. M. Balden, who typed the lectures as they were modified after one delivery and before the next, to my wife who typed the final manuscript, and to Mr. Steven MacArthur and the Reverend Thomas G. Allen who assisted me with proofreading.

1
scripture

It would seem proper to begin by defining the nature of preaching but it is more logical to begin with the nature of Scripture for preaching has to do with the understanding and interpretation of Scripture and the way we understand and interpret Scripture is controlled by what we think Scripture is. While there might have been agreement among Christians on the nature of Scripture two hundred years ago, today there are many views. Each view, linked to a theory of interpretation, might produce a different understanding of the place of Scripture in preaching.

Without attempting an exclusive list we give a few of the options: (1) If we believe that all Scripture must have a meaning for today then we may be forced like Origen to allegorize at least some parts of it in order to bring out that relevance. Origen did this with those passages which contained theological statements which were unacceptable, e.g. anthropomorphisms, or moral statements which quite clearly fell below the standards of Christ. (2) If Scripture is considered to consist of testimony to the great acts of God then preaching will always endeavor to get behind Scripture to the original acts and preaching will proceed not so much from the statements in Scripture as from the acts of God which are considered to lie behind it; in the New Testament a great deal of emphasis will then be put on what Jesus actually said and did. (3) If Scripture is considered to consist of a series of statements of revealed truth there will be no compulsion to go back to the historical act (it will normally be considered as having happened as described); the statements will be taken as theological propositions which the sermon assumes still to be true in the situation of today and applies to that situation. (4) A view of Scripture which regards parts of it as theologically and morally inadequate or as unacceptable to a modern scientific view of the world may lead to these portions being set aside and rarely, if ever, being used in preaching. These are only a few of the possible options and it would be easy to pick on others. There is no need to outline them all; it is more important to go on to sketch briefly the conception which will be used in this book and which, it is believed, accords best with contemporary biblical scholarship.

The New Testament did not just suddenly appear in its present form. When we examine it, it reveals clues to its own evolution. There lies behind it a considerable process of growth of tradition. This is quite apparent when its writers quote existing statements of belief or use existing hymns. Amongst the earliest of the former is that in 1 Corinthians 15:3–5 where Paul says he is employing tradition:

> Christ died for our sins in accordance with the scriptures,
> he was buried,
> he was raised on the third day in accordance with the scriptures,
> he appeared to Cephas, then to the twelve,

and of the latter the hymn of Philippians 2:6–11. But it is not only the quotation of previous creeds and hymns within Scripture which shows the growth of tradition, the Gospels show it even more clearly. Most scholars see a three-fold, if not four-fold, development in Mark 4:1–20. Here we can certainly attribute to Mark the introduction which sets the scene by the lake and the reference to Jesus teaching many things in parables (vss. 1,2). Probably we should also attribute to him the very difficult verses in the middle (vss. 10–12) which assert that the secret of the kingdom has been given to believers but that for those outside everything is in parables so that they should not be saved, though Mark may well have been adding in a piece of tradition. To the activity of the church prior to Mark we attribute the interpretation of the parable which equates the various soils with men (vss. 14–20). The parable itself goes back to Jesus. Thus we have the first stage in which Jesus told the story; the second, in which its meaning being lost, it is given an interpretation to make it suitable for use in the early communities; then, thirdly, a general theory of parables is created out of the conflict between the original story and the interpretation; and finally the whole is set back again into the life of Jesus. This is an example of growth both before Mark wrote and in his composition. That there is also development after Mark can be seen from the modifications Matthew and Luke make in Mark. Luke modifies a statement like Mark's, "He who endures to the end will be saved" (13:13), into, "By your endurance you will gain your lives" (21:19) because he is more certain than Mark that the End is not going to arrive fairly immediately. Matthew modifies Mark's account of Jesus' baptism by John by adding an explanation for it: apparently a baptism of Jesus for the remission of sins caused difficulty or it was felt necessary to stress Jesus' superiority over John; so Matthew makes John say to Jesus, " 'I need to be baptized by you, and do you come to me?' " and Jesus answer, " 'Let it be so now; for thus it is fitting for us to fulfil all righteousness.' " (Matt. 3:14–15) Modifications did not cease with Matthew and Luke; what we know of the later apocryphal gospels shows that they continued the same process. The very story of the baptism of Jesus is further modified in the Gospel of the Nazaraeans; while Jesus is still at home his mother and brothers say to him: "John the Baptist baptizes unto the remission of sins; let us go and be baptized by him." But he said to them, "Wherein have I sinned that I should go and be baptized by him? Unless what I have said is ignorance (a sin of ignorance)."[1] And modifications have gone on continually since then; it is only necessary to listen to almost any preacher who chooses a Gospel incident as the center of his sermon to become aware of this.

But the tradition has also developed in other ways. During the first few centuries views about the nature of the person of Christ and of his relation to the Father were continually modified. If we speak of Father and Son then we need to define exactly what we mean in order to avoid false conclusions that could be drawn from the use of a metaphor; thus the strong element of subordination which we find in the Gospel of John is eventually ironed out. Without following the development of the biblical tradition through the centuries up to now it is sufficient to reiterate that it has been taking place.

There is a sense in which tradition is a steady flow from Jesus to

our time: in that flow there are continual modifications to meet changing circumstances. Yet it would be wrong to think of it as one current
flowing simply and straightforwardly from the beginning until now;
at the beginning the current divided and the flow has gone in different
directions; often the divided currents cross one another or rejoin and
interact with one another. What this means will become clearer as we
go on. Of this flow of tradition we possess, as it were, cross-sections,
or perhaps a more appropriate metaphor might be to say that at
certain points the flow becomes "frozen," not that its frozen nature
stopped the flow but that we have access to it at certain points; at these
it is as if the flow were frozen; we see it as it was at those points. The
writings of Barth or Calvin, of Augustine or Thomas Aquinas represent such "freezings" of the tradition. So in a more summary fashion
do the creeds of the church. In all these, tradition is as it were
momentarily trapped and we can see it. Scripture is the earliest written form of such freezing of the tradition.

But it is wrong to think of the New Testament as *a* freezing of the
tradition; the New Testament contains a number of freezings which
took place at different times and under varying circumstances. These
freezings are a mixed bag of writings of various genres, Gospels,
letters, revelations of the End, by various authors with varying social
and educational backgrounds, and from various dates, with perhaps
as much as eighty years between the first and last writings.

At this point it is necessary to introduce three terms which will
be used frequently and which need to be defined so that they can be
kept separate from each other. These terms are: situation, culture,
world-view. By *situation* is meant the actual circumstances which call
out a New Testament writing; these will be circumstances both in the
life of the writer and in the community to which he writes. The
situation of 1 Corinthians is what was taking place in Corinth; Paul
had learned of these events through a letter from Corinth and through
a visit by some of the church leaders. He was also influenced by what
was happening to him in Ephesus where, for instance, he may have
had to suffer some persecution. The situation of Romans consists of
these elements: the nature of the church there, the successful outcome
of the struggle against the Judaizers in Galatia, Paul's proposed jour-
ney to Jerusalem with the collection and a possible confrontation with
the Christian leaders in that church. Often the situation is difficult to

determine. In 1 John it is clearly that of some community or communities affected by a gnostic or docetic heresy, but we know nothing of the writer.

The second term is *culture*. This is the total situation of the writer and recipients expressed in terms of the prevailing concepts and ideas to which life on the whole conforms itself. There were two clear cultures in the world of the New Testament—the Jewish and the Hellenistic. They had begun to penetrate one another, or, more precisely, Hellenism had begun to enter Palestine so that a purely Jewish culture no longer existed; Jewish culture however had not affected Hellenism to any great extent. But despite this interpenetration they can still be adequately distinguished.

The third term is *world-view*. It is related to culture but it is not the same. It is more personal. Within any culture there will be a number of possible world-views. World-view approximates to a man's personal philosophy or theology. Within Hellenism there were the world-views of the Stoic, the Epicurean, the Neo-Platonist, the Cynic; a gnostic world-view began to appear in the first century. Within Judaism we find those of the wise man, the apocalypticist, the nationalist. In a sense everyone has a world-view of his own; but this is not to say that everyone has a philosophy or theology of his own or that everyone's world-view is self-consistent; everyone has a standpoint from which he looks at life, or, more correctly for most people, he has a number of standpoints which he adopts at different times under different circumstances. Together these add up to his world-view. We should note that these three ideas, situation, culture, and world-view, are not wholly separable concepts but flow into one another. Moreover not every world-view is compatible with every culture—the apocalyptic does not easily fit into Hellenistic culture.

Alongside the world-views mentioned we can speak of a *Christian world-view*, meaning one which Christians shared; it differs from all the others. It was critical of both Hellenistic and Jewish cultures, though necessarily it partook in varying proportions of both. Equally it might be termed the Christian *sub-culture*, where *sub* is used, not to indicate a culture subordinate to Judaism or Hellenism, but the culture held by the sub-group of Christians within Jewish and Hellenistic culture.

We return now to our discussion of the tradition we find in Scripture. Any freezing of tradition takes place in a situation, in a culture, through the world-view of the writer of that particular piece of the New Testament and as a part of the Christian world-view or sub-culture. This can be put in another way with another image. When a chemist pours one solution into another in a test tube and leaves it crystals may result; if he begins with one solution and pours it into a number of different other solutions there may result a number of types of crystals, but the crystals within each test tube will be the same. The solution which is poured in is the flowing or moving tradition; the solution into which it is poured is the combination of situation, culture, and world-view of the writer and readers; the result is a New Testament writing. If any of the elements of situation, culture, or world-view is varied the result will be varied—and of course these elements are varied in the different parts of the New Testament.

It must also be realized that just the fact that a "freezing" has taken place affects the flow of tradition. The freezings are not just the dial readings which a scientist observes and which do not affect his experiment. When a freezing takes place this itself exercises a control-ling factor on what has flowed into the freezing and flows out beyond it; thus any freezing tends to control later freezings. The freezing which we term the Gospel of Mark affected the later freezings which we term the Gospels of Matthew and Luke.

Within the New Testament there are thus a number of freezings or precipitations. Some of these are apparently continuous with one another. 1 Corinthians 15:3–5 lies within the greater precipitation of Paul's letter to the Corinthians and the two are not in contradiction with one another. Matthew may be said to be in continuity with Mark, though quite clearly there are points where Matthew qualifies and varies Mark; this is presumably either because the current of tradition which flows through Mark encountered in Matthew another current of tradition and the two have interacted or because the situation, culture, and world-view of Matthew and his readers led to variation in the precipitate. But there are instances where we cannot see any continuity; for example, there is no direct line between John and Mark if we assume, as most scholars do today, that Mark was not known to John. The line which runs through Mark and the line which runs through John divided at some point earlier than both. There is equally no direct line between John and Paul; we have separate precipitations of different streams of tradition. But the same stream of tradition may produce precipitations which differ even in the same writer. Thus there are differences in the way the End is viewed in Paul's writings; at first he sees it as coming in his own lifetime; later he is less clear about this.

Even concrete elements of the tradition will appear as precipitates in different ways. The parable of the shepherd and the lost sheep when it appears in Luke (15:3–7) sets out God as one who seeks the lost but when it appears in Matthew (18:10–14) it is a call to pastors not to neglect their duty towards the sheep of their congregations.[2] The passion story is precipitated in two different chronological settings in Mark and in John. In Mark Jesus eats the Passover before he is betrayed; in John the Passover has still not been eaten when Jesus is dead (see 13:1, 18:28, 19:31), and so Jesus can be presented as the Passover lamb. The reasons for this difference need not detain us; it is sufficient that it has occurred. When we leave factual material of this type and turn instead to the more complex material of the tradition dealing with theological view the problem becomes more complex.

We shall examine four areas in which through variations in culture, situation, and world-view we encounter different crystalizations, precipitates, or freezings.

(1) In the New Testament the issue of variation in theological interpretation to which attention has been most often drawn is that between Paul and James. Since Luther refused to put the Letter of James on the same level as most of the remainder of the New Testament and spoke of it as an epistle of straw it has continued to be attacked, though many have attempted to defend it. The discussion has centered on the meaning of faith in the two writers. It is very difficult to be certain about the original situation of the Letter; it is probably easiest to suppose that it represents a response to a misunderstood Paulinism in which it was argued that faith is sufficient to save a man, and in which that faith was intellectually conceived, i.e., it was not obedient trust as in Paul, but belief in certain propositions about Christ and God. James is quite clear that such a faith does not

save, but in denying this does he go too far on the other side when he writes "Was not Abraham our father justified by works, when he offered his son Isaac upon the altar?" (2:21) For Paul, Abraham was clearly not justified by works; works follow on faith and faith which does not result in works denies itself and is therefore not faith; it is not an inadequate kind of faith, but not faith at all. For James being a Christian consists in having the right belief about God and carrying through the law of love. That we find here a different conception of religion from Paul's comes out clearly in James' definition of what religion is:

> Religion that is pure and undefiled before God and the Father is this: to visit orphans and widows in their affliction, and to keep oneself unstained from the world. (1:27)

This may not be a full definition of religion but it emphasizes that it consists in ethical behavior, and assumes a belief in the existence of God as we learn elsewhere in the epistle. It does not seem likely that Paul would have agreed with this, though he would certainly have agreed that the Christian ought to visit orphans and widows. In a situation of a misunderstood Paulinism this is the way in which Christianity has precipitated itself.[3]

(2) Let us now pick the teaching on a particular issue as it appears in a number of writers—the issue of the attitude of the Christian to the state. At first sight it would look as if we ought to be able to obtain a unified doctrine from the New Testament on such a clear-cut issue. The standard passage is Romans 13:1–7:

> Let every person be subject to the governing authorities. For there is no authority except from God, and those that exist have been instituted by God. Therefore he who resists the authorities resists what God has appointed, and those who resist will incur judgment. (13:1–2)

Similar teaching is found in 1 Peter 2:13–17:

> Be subject for the Lord's sake to every human institution, whether it be to the emperor as supreme, or to governors as sent by him to punish those who do wrong and to praise those who do right. (2:13–14)

In both these passages it is assumed that the civil authorities have been appointed by God and that therefore they will administer justice fairly. But there is a different picture in Revelation; here Rome is termed Babylon, the code name of the Jew for everything earthly that is evil:

> The woman was arrayed in purple and scarlet, and bedecked with gold and jewels and pearls, holding in her hand a golden cup full of abominations and the impurities of her fornication; and on her forehead was written a name of mystery: "Babylon the great, mother of harlots and of earth's abominations." And I saw the woman, drunk with the blood of the saints and the blood of the martyrs of Jesus. (17:4–6)

That which Romans and 1 Peter view as good and as instituted by God for men's good is now viewed as diabolical. But we begin to get this even in Paul:

> None of the rulers of this age understood this; for if they had, they would not have crucified the Lord of glory. (1 Cor. 2:8)

It is probable that there is a double reference in "the rulers of this age"; they are both the earthly rulers like Pilate and the High Priest and are the spiritual powers. We probably find the same inconsistency in 1 Peter when we compare 2:13–17 with 5:13 when the city, Rome, from which the letter is written is termed Babylon. This is true also of the trial scene in John's Gospel where Pilate debates the issue with Jesus. On the one hand Pilate is said by Jesus to have his authority from God: " 'You would have no power over me unless it had been given you from above' "; (19:11) on the other hand the whole Passion is viewed as influenced by Satan: after Judas had received the morsel of bread from Jesus, Satan entered into him, and Pilate, unable to resist the tide of events which begins with this, becomes Satan's tool in the death of Jesus. That the ruling authorities may be hostile to Christianity is already seen in Acts, though without the demonic overtones we have just observed. When Peter and John are brought before the Sanhedrin and commanded not to teach about Jesus, Peter replies " 'We must obey God rather than men.' " (Acts 5:29) He cannot then have regarded the Jewish ruling authorities as appointed by God and so to be obeyed under all circumstances. There is no need to explore the reason for these varying attitudes towards the state other than to suggest that they arose out of the different situations of the church and of the New Testament writers. In part also they had their roots in Judaism.

While it appears quite reasonable that with changing governments there should appear differing attitudes to the state, what we have detected is not different attitudes on the part of men but different views on the place of the state in God's administration of the world. It is not just practical attitudes towards the state which change but views of the place of the state in God's economy, a much more fundamental matter. These varying views, however, have been affected by the differing circumstances of the writers and readers of the New Testament.

(3) Our next example is drawn from the religious rather than the ethical field. The first Christians believed the world was not going to endure for long: Jesus would soon reappear and God would establish his Kingdom in all its perfection. Thus in a letter as late as Romans we find Paul writing "salvation is nearer to us now than when we first believed"; (13:11) if the world is going to last thousands of years then the few years between when the Roman Christians first believed and when Paul writes are not significant and there would be no point in mentioning them. We meet the same concept of the nearness of the End in many other places in Paul:

> For this we declare to you by the word of the Lord, that we who are alive, who are left until the coming of the Lord, shall not precede those who have fallen asleep. (1 Thess. 4:15)

> Now these things happened to them as a warning, but they were written down for our instruction, upon whom the end of the ages has come. (1 Cor. 10:11)

Paul believed that he himself was living in the final days of the world and might indeed be alive when the End came. He was wrong; the End did not come and Christians had to live with the concept of a world which might continue indefinitely. The author of 2 Peter saw the problem and attempted to wriggle out of it:

> First of all you must understand this, that scoffers will come in the last days with scoffing, following their own passions and saying, "Where is the promise of his coming? For ever since the fathers fell asleep, all things have continued as they were from the beginning of creation." (3:3–4)

The answer is twofold:

> But do not ignore this one fact, beloved, that with the Lord one day is
> a thousand years, and a thousand years as one day. The Lord is not slow
> about his promise as some count slowness, but is forbearing toward you,
> not wishing that any should perish, but that all should reach repentance.
> (3:8–9)

God's idea of nearness is different from man's and he stretches out
time so that all may have a better chance to repent. We find a similar
change in respect to the expectancy of the End when we move from
Mark to Luke; Luke modifies the Markan form of the sayings of Jesus
to accommodate them to an indefinitely long period before the parousia; Luke still believes there will be a parousia but he does not
think it is imminent. Mark 9:1,

> "Truly, I say to you, there are some standing here who will not taste
> death before they see that the kingdom of God has come with power,"

becomes in Luke 9:27,

> "But I tell you truly, there are some standing here who will not taste
> death before they see the kingdom of God."

By omitting "has come with power" Luke has made the saying time-
less; to "see the kingdom" may now mean to perceive its inward
nature and not refer to the kingdom which comes at Christ's return.
Mark 13:21 (cf. Matt. 24:23),

> "And then if any one says to you, 'Look, here is the Christ!' or 'Look,
> there he is!' do not believe it,"

is set in the context of the expectation of the End; in Luke 17:20–21
this context disappears:

> Being asked by the Pharisees when the kingdom of God was coming,
> he answered them, "The kingdom of God is not coming with signs to
> be observed; nor will they say, 'Lo, here it is!' or 'There!' for behold, the
> kingdom of God is in the midst of you."

In effect Luke says: do not look for the parousia but look for the
kingdom within (either within the community or within the individual). We say that the situation has changed but we do so thinking not

of the situation in the sense of a localized situation in some particular
Christian community but of the total situation of the church; and the
alteration in the situation of the church has not come from the condition of the world outside but from its own better understanding of the
End produced in it by the passage of time.

(4) We turn from this to something which appears to affect more
directly the center of Christian faith: there are striking differences in
the way in which salvation is presented in the Gospels. (a) In Mark
salvation is seen under two aspects. In the first place there is a victory in Jesus over Satan and the demonic world; witness the exorcism stories which are emphasized more in this Gospel than in the
others. In the second place Jesus' death is a victory over sin; witness
the ransom saying,

> "For the Son of man also came not to be served but to serve, and to
> give his life as a ransom for many," (10:45)

which comes at a turning point in the Gospel when Jesus is just about
to enter Jerusalem. The life of the disciple is also to be related directly
to the cross. Each of the three predictions by Jesus of his death (8:31;
9:31; 10:33–34) is followed by teaching on the nature of discipleship.
This teaching is not in the ordinary sense moral or ethical teaching
but is more basic; it is typified by the verses that follow the first
prediction:

> "If any man would come after me, let him deny himself and take up
> his cross and follow me. For whoever would save his life will lose it;
> and whoever loses his life for my sake and the gospel's will save it."
> (8:34–35)

What is demanded is not just behavior in accordance with a norm,
even the norm of love, but the denial of the self, the readiness for a
person to lose what he believes to be the very essence of his being;
nothing he himself can do will save him; efforts in that direction only
lead to loss of his real being.

(b) When we turn to Matthew we find a subtle change. Matthew
retains all that Mark has said about the redemptive significance of the
death of Jesus, though there is not so much stress on Jesus' victory
over Satan; however he has added a vast quantity of Jesus' teaching

on behavior and so has brought ethical behavior into the forefront of his picture. Most significant here is the concluding "great commission," which most scholars today regard as a Matthean creation:

> Jesus . . . said to them, "All authority in heaven and on earth has been given to me. Go therefore and make disciples of all nations, baptizing them in the name of the Father and of the Son and of the Holy Spirit, teaching them to observe all that I have commanded you; and lo, I am with you always, to the close of the age." (28:18–20)

In making disciples the emphasis does not lie on calling men to repentance but on teaching them the sayings of Jesus with which, as we have seen, Matthew has filled his Gospel. Christians have a new law, the law of love, which stands forever and which must be observed. It is in the light of this that we read passages like

> "For truly, I say to you, till heaven and earth pass away, not an iota, not a dot, will pass from the law until all is accomplished. Whoever then relaxes one of the least of these commandments and teaches men so, shall be called least in the kingdom of heaven; but he who does them and teaches them shall be called great in the kingdom of heaven." (5:18,19)

This does not refer to the Jewish law but to the Christian law of love as the exposition in the following chapters of the Sermon on the Mount shows. Matthew is not presenting Jesus here to those outside the church and saying that to become Christians they must keep the law of love; he is writing to believers. This is not a simple doctrine of works, yet works enter. Matthew repeatedly draws attention to the Last Judgment and this is made according to works, but they are the works of believers. We may suppose that Matthew was faced with a new situation in which the church was expanding and in which there were many members who did not live up to the law of love; he needs to warn them in order to preserve the purity of the community. So he stresses obedience to the law. In summary his position runs like this: Christ has died for you and borne your sins; keep his law and you will be saved when God comes to judge, for he will judge you by your life.

(c) When we turn to Luke the picture again changes. Luke drops passages like the ransom saying and while he stresses the need for repentance he does not link this directly to the death of Jesus. Thus Peter on the day of Pentecost proclaims:

> "Repent, and be baptized every one of you in the name of Jesus Christ for the forgiveness of your sins; and you shall receive the gift of the Holy Spirit." (Acts 2:38)

Jesus' death is of course part of God's plan of redemption, but forgiveness comes through repentance. It is because of this that Luke can tell the story of the prodigal son in which God receives the sinner without any allusion to the death of Jesus and that the tax gatherer can be said to go down from the temple justified because he has acknowledged his sin. This is negative. Luke however does give a more positive place to Jesus: for him, much more than for Matthew or Mark, Jesus has become men's example. (It is remarkable how little his behavior as example is set out in the rest of the New Testament.) First, Jesus is portrayed as the proto-martyr; close parallels are drawn between the death of Stephen and that of Jesus: when Isaiah 53 is cited in the story of the Ethiopian eunuch it is not to depict Jesus as a sacrifice for men but as example. Secondly, Jesus is portrayed as a man filled by the Spirit; time and again the Spirit is mentioned in the first two chapters of the Gospel; there are many more references to Jesus as being led by the Spirit in the remainder of Luke than in Matthew or Mark (Luke 4:1, two references to Mark's one [1:12]; Luke 4:14, no reference in Mark [1:14] or Matthew [4:12]; Luke 10:21 [cf. Matt. 11:25]); in the programmatic sermon in the synagogue in Nazareth Jesus describes himself as the one on whom the Spirit is:

> "The Spirit of the Lord is upon me, because he has anointed me to preach good news to the poor." (4:18)

Thirdly, Jesus is portrayed as a man of prayer much more than in the other Gospels; at his baptism and transfiguration it is only in Luke that he is depicted as praying, and the same is true of the time Peter confesses him at Caesarea Philippi. Thus Jesus functions as martyr, as Spirit-filled man, as man of prayer, and he is depicted in this way to help Christians who have to face martyrdom, temptation, and pagan immorality. So we see that Jesus and the Gospel are presented in three different ways in the three Synoptic Gospels.

(d) The picture again changes when we turn to the Gospel of John. Certainly Jesus is still depicted as men's redeemer in the traditional way which relates him to them as one who deals with their sin. He is the Lamb of God who takes away the sin of the world (1:29). But he appears even more as Revealer—he redeems through revelation and, though the revelation he gives is more than just intellectual revelation, he is primarily Revealer. We can see this in the new range of predicates which are applied to him: he is the light of the world, the truth, the way, the Logos. It is seen even more in the long discourses of the Gospel. Their purpose is no longer to instruct men in what it means to love one's neighbor, as is the case in so much of the teaching in Matthew and Luke, but to disclose Jesus' nature and through that to disclose the nature of God: "He who has seen me has seen the Father." (14:9) It is in this Gospel that his divine nature and his pre-existence are set out most openly but always in relation to the Father. He knows the Father, the Father knows him and both would have men know them. In the course of this there begins to be developed the Christology which eventually led to the great creeds of the church. If Paul is the great expounder of the death of Christ, John is that of his incarnation.

Clearly some of the teaching of the New Testament books is difficult to reconcile with other bits; clearly some of it is just different in emphasis, a difference produced by differing situations and cultures. But what is it that is presented differently? What is it, to return to an earlier image, which is precipitated? What is the tradition of which we have the "freezings"? It was customary some years ago to stress the unity of the New Testament. New Testament scholars no longer do this, yet surely there must be something which holds the Christian movement together and allows a distinction to be made between what is Christian and what is heretical.

We could begin by trying to isolate some central form of Christian teaching and think of it as that which is precipitated. It does not need to be something which is set down in actual words in the New Testament, but something which comprises what is common to all the New Testament writings, say the Nicene Creed; but at once we run into difficulty: the Nicene Creed excludes a genuine subordination of the Son to the Father, and yet in the Gospel of John we repeatedly find this. On the other hand if we strip our basic faith-statement down to a simple sentence in language drawn from the New Testament there are still difficulties. We might choose a statement like "Jesus died and rose again so that men's sins might be forgiven," but we have seen that while Luke does emphasize forgiveness he links it to repentance rather than the death of Jesus. If we make it still simpler and say "God has through Jesus done everything that needs to be done for our redemption," are we really saying very much? "Redemption" is in any case a word highly charged with theology and it is only as we expand it that the sentence takes meaning, and as we expand it we run into the kind of difficulties that arise out of detailed statements; it is always possible to pick a bit of the New Testament for which any such statement is not the norm.

Perhaps, though, we could isolate one central doctrine which would give us the essence of the Christian faith. Luther thought he could do this and he isolated justification by faith; in its light he judged the New Testament documents and had some very hard things to say about the Letter of James. No matter what doctrine we isolate we shall always find that we have to omit some part of the New Testament because it does not conform to it. The same is quite clearly true if we isolate one writer of the New Testament and allow him to dominate our interpretation. Most Protestant thought has allowed itself to use Paul as a norm; Catholic thought has always been happier with Matthew, Anglican with John.[4] In practice those who pick a central principle or doctrine have rarely been as honest as Luther; they have simply ignored the bits that did not fit with their chosen center rather than denying them Christian status.

But does not the New Testament itself provide ways of stating the central kerygma of the faith? Do we not find in it little creeds which would suffice for our purpose? Yet when we examine them we find that they have differing emphases: it is sufficient to state a few to see this.

Jesus is the Christ (Mark 8:29)

seems unexceptionable but Mark regards this as an inadequate formula, for Messiah (=Christ) is a difficult term for Gentile Christians; it is a Jewish term without a genuine parallel in a Hellenistic world; so he replaces it with Jesus as Son of God.

Paul's summary of the gospel as he had preached it in Thessalonica provides another example:

> how you turned to God from idols, to serve a living and true God, and to wait for his Son from heaven, whom he raised from the dead, Jesus who delivers us from the wrath to come. (1 Thess. 1:9–10)

There is no reference here to redemption from sin which many would consider the essence of Christianity and there is too much emphasis on idolatory for it to be of any use to those who have never seen an idol used in worship, and that means most of Western Christendom.

Perhaps the one which would be favored by most traditional Christians is the best known of them all:

> Christ died for our sins in accordance with the scriptures,
> he was buried;
> he was raised on the third day in accordance with the scriptures,
> he appeared to Cephas, then to the twelve. (1 Cor. 15:3–5)

But this has no reference to Christ's victory over sin or the devil; this, however, is found in the Philippian hymn (2:6–11) and in the many credal passages which refer to his ascension:

> (Christ) who has gone into heaven and is at the right hand of God, with angels, authorities, and powers subject to him. (1 Peter 3:22)

This victory over the supernatural powers, whether evil or good, was an essential part of the New Testament faith. There is then no primitive creed or kerygmatic statement which by itself solves our problem as the real essential which is precipitated.[5] The essential can only be Jesus himself; this is why the religion of his followers is called Christianity. But does this get us much further? We cannot draw up a clear and defined picture of Jesus and then say "Crystallize this out in your situation and you will have the meaning of Christianity for it." For all we have to begin with are different crystallizations. We only have access to this Jesus who is precipitated through the precipitations which we possess; we have no direct access. It was the illusion of the liberal movement in theology that Jesus could be reconstructed, as it were, and that through that reconstruction we could reach the essence of Christianity. Now it is certainly true that there is much that can be learnt about Jesus from the New Testament: that he lived and taught in Galilee; that he died in Jerusalem by crucifixion. But when we look into the New Testament we find that all these statements about him come to us already covered with meaning; they carry with them their interpretation. They have been drawn up by people who saw him, not as an objective Palestinian reporter might have seen him as he went about in Galilee, but as those who believe he rose from the dead. Their reports come from this side of the resurrection and are colored by the understanding it gave them of him as Son of God and their Lord. Thus every event in his life takes on a richer meaning. It was not enough for them to say, "Jesus died"; they had to go on and say, "Jesus died in accordance with God's plan," or "Jesus died for our sins," or offer some other such interpretation. We cannot isolate, as it were, a neutral picture of Jesus which will control our interpretation. All we possess are interpretations; and the interpretations are phrased in the cultures of the writers, colored by their world-views and precipitated by their situations.

Most of us if we look back will admit that our understanding of Christianity has often been deepened, not so much by reading Scripture, but by hearing sermons and lectures and reading modern Christian and sometimes even non-Christian authors. There has been a crystallization in their words which has made us appreciate our faith because it was expressed in the modes of thought to which we are accustomed in our ordinary lives. The authority of Scripture is, therefore, not so immediately important for the practical development of the Christian life as is sometimes alleged.

As we have seen there was a development in Christian thinking prior to the writing of the New Testament books and there was development after their writing; why should the particular precipitation which is the New Testament be all-important? The traditional answer was that the New Testament was written by apostolic men, mostly those who had been in direct contact with Jesus. Few New Testament scholars today would accept that as a description of those who wrote the New Testament. But most New Testament scholars would not change the selection of books which form our New Testament. This raises a major issue which has been the center of a lively discussion in the last few years: why a New Testament canon? It is unfortunately impossible to give space to it here.

We have discovered differences in the understanding of Christianity in the New Testament. Few who have studied the New Testament will be surprised at this. How can we account for these differences? It may be said that if the New Testament consists of a set of precipitations of Christ this is like a set of photographs of a cathedral taken from different angles; because the building is three-dimensional and the photographs are two-dimensional no single photograph can fully disclose the structure of the building. We must take a number together to build up a full picture; similarly Christ is greater than any single description of him, and we need the variety we have in the New Testament. While this image is helpful there are two aspects in which it is seriously inadequate. (a) Whereas we can go round and round the cathedral taking more and more photographs to build up our picture if we find we have not already taken enough, we have only a limited number of precipitations of Jesus in the New Testament; we can give no guarantee that every angle has been covered; indeed we may suspect that many have not been. (b) It is not just true to say that the precipitations complement one another as the photographs may do; the precipitations, as we have already seen, at times come very close to contradicting one another even if they do not actually do so. But this is not surprising. Each of those who gives us his precipitation in the New Testament was not merely limited in understanding but sinful. It is as if the camera had a distorting lens as well as being limited to taking two-dimensional photographs. But it is worse; given only one camera we might with experience make out some of the nature of the distortion in the lens, but in fact each precipitation comes, as it were, through a different camera with a lens distorting in a different way. It is very difficult to find out about the nature of the distortion because we know so little of the writers. As his letters show Paul could be both over-sensitive to criticism and over-bearing: knowing this we can make some allowance when he prays that the disturbers of his Galatian churches may go to hell; but was he too keen to develop an apostolic authority for himself which ran counter to Jesus' conception of ministry through service? Different scholars read this differently. But if we can make allowances for this element in our interpretation of Paul because we have several of his letters and an account in Acts, we know nothing of the character of the writers of the letter of James or the first Gospel other than what we can learn from the writings themselves. Differences in the expression of Christianity, even seemingly contradictory differences, are not of themselves a necessary drawback to the interpretation of what God is saying to us through Scripture; indeed as the sequel unfolds we may see that they are positive gain for they at least prevent us from making too simple a transference of what is in Scripture to our present situation.

What of the inspiration of Scripture? In the light of the argument that has been made we must rule out any form of infallible inspiration. Equally, we must rule out any idea that it took place in an ecstasy or frenzy in which the writers were overwhelmed and became passive instruments; the biblical writers were always fully in possession of their mental faculties; they knew what they were writing, even if they did not always express themselves as gracefully or as correctly as they, and we, would have wished. Nor can we allow that the Spirit wrote into their words some hidden meaning which later readers would discover but of which the original writers were unaware. Many people seem to have the rather crude conception of God feeding thoughts and ideas into the mind of the writer; after passing through his mind and being phrased in his human language they appear as the words of Scripture. We cannot be happy with such an image; if anyone wants to retain it, it must be said that the minds which the thoughts and ideas passed through were limited and sinful and left on the material the impression of limitation and sin. Keeping within the biblical terminology it is better to begin from Paul's conception of the gifts of the Spirit. In recent years much popular attention has been given to the gifts of tongues and of healing but less to two of the other gifts he lists in the same passage, viz., the gifts of the utterance of wisdom and knowledge. We might say that the writers of Scripture had these gifts and through them were led to an understanding of Christ, which they were led to formulate in words. John in his Gospel speaks of the Spirit as leading men to truth. This is the same idea. The precipitations which we call Scripture are the result of these gifts. If we accept this view then it must also be acknowledged that the gifts still continue; the interpreter of Scripture depends on the same gifts from the same Spirit. That the writers of Scripture had these gifts does not mean that the world-view and the culture in which a particular writer wrote were eliminated; but the world-view is one that has itself been modified by the Spirit in the understanding that the writer has received and the culture in which he lives is now seen as a culture that is only partly of God. This also means that the differences between the precipitations must not be over-stated; it is the one Spirit whose gift is given to all the writers; together they belonged to the one church, held a largely common world-view, and experienced the one Christ, even if they expressed that experience differently. But must not what has been said here of the writers of Scripture not also be said of many of its great interpreters? Did not Augustine and Luther, Bonhoeffer and Aquinas receive these gifts of the Spirit so that they understood and expressed their understanding in the terms of their own situation and culture?

It may be said that this view of Scripture is wholly relativistic. Is there no absolute in Scripture? Is Scripture itself not an absolute? The view propounded here is relativistic in the sense that Scripture is not an absolute, nor is any portion of it an absolute; it is not relativistic in the sense that that of which Scripture is a freezing, or a number of freezings, is not an absolute. The absolute is the Word and not the words, or, to put it differently, the absolute is Jesus Christ and not the stories about him or the interpretations of him which we find in the New Testament. If it is said that the absolute is Jesus Christ this does not mean that we can unearth from the New Testament a series of facts about Jesus—that he was born, healed a certain paralytic, told the parable of the sower, was arrested and crucified, and that he rose from the dead. The absolute is not the history of the earthly Jesus; yet without the earthly Jesus there would be no absolute. Nor is the absolute a fixed, final, and irreducible interpretation of the significance; as we have seen we can never reach such; even if we could it would always be expressed differently in different cultures; there is no interpretation which can be freed from its culture and stated in such a way as to apply to all cultures. To go back to the earlier image of the cathedral; we may have only a limited number of photographs, none of them may be perfect, and yet we do not doubt its existence. The absolute is there though the interpretations may be inadequate. There is sufficient similarity between the photographs to assure us we are dealing with the same building; there is sufficient similarity between the various crystallizations of which Scripture consists to assure us that we are dealing with the same Christ. It is Jesus, the risen Jesus, who holds the New Testament together.

It is this book, the New Testament, with its different and sometimes contradictory views but of which each part reflects an understanding of the one Christ, which lies at the basis of our Christian faith; it is this book which every Christian wishes to interpret in its relevance to himself and for whose interpretation he desires from the Spirit the gifts of understanding and wisdom so that he may both understand and express what he understands. And yet it is not the book itself which the interpreter ultimately interprets, but the Jesus whom the book interprets. He does not set out to adapt the book to his situation so that its message may speak to him; he seeks instead to bring Jesus into his situation. He does not set out to think the thoughts of the New Testament writers over again, but through them to listen to the Word of God. Because they are the primary place where that Word speaks he must keep them central.

2
OUR WORLD

We ended the last chapter with a position which regarded Scripture as consisting of a number of precipitations or crystallizations of Christ; precipitations into different cultures in different situations by people who had different world-views. Our culture, many of our situations, much of our world-view are different from all of those of the New Testament. Perhaps that does not need to be proved. For the moment one example will suffice; by choosing an extreme case it will easily be seen how much is involved. It is a very well-known example. How is the lamb of God to be explained to an Eskimo?[1] This problem first arose acutely for those translating the Bible into the languages of the Eskimo since there is no word for lamb in those languages. What is worse, there is no equivalent concept. It is possible to render the "lamb of God" by the "baby seal of God"; but the seal occupies a different place in the mind of an Eskimo from that which the lamb did in the mind of a Palestinian of Jesus' day. The seal only exists to be hunted, its flesh for food, its skin for clothing; it is never fed or cared for. The lamb may be killed eventually for food and clothing; but someone, the shepherd, has looked after it from its birth; he has given it a name and has led it from pasture to pasture even though in the end he may eat it[2] or bring it to the temple as a sacrifice. For the Eskimo there is no seal-herd; "the Lord's my seal-herd" is an impossible thought; the seal is not an object for sacrifice to God nor the center of a Paschal feast. The affectionate relationship of the shepherd for his sheep, seen in the way he gives them pet names, is unknown to the Eskimo in his attitude towards seals. The difference

between the Eskimo and the Palestinian goes further than this; it is
the difference between an agricultural and pastoral culture and a
fishing and hunting culture. Can what is expressed in the agricultural
and pastoral culture ever be translated satisfactorily into the other?
(In passing we should note that we do not live in an agricultural
culture any longer; even the farmer who keeps his animals and fowl
in "factory" conditions rather than in their natural environment has
moved considerably from such a culture into an industrial and scientific culture.) If there are things in Scripture which are outside any
possible life-style for an Eskimo, will this not also be true for us?
Essentially that is the problem. In one way at least our position may
not be as difficult as that of the Eskimo; our culture is continuous with
that of Scripture because of the way Western civilization has developed. The culture of the Eskimo has no continuity with that of ancient
Israel; yet because of the absence of technological advance it may be
closer to it in other ways than ours, for as the centuries have gone by
the effect of Israelite culture on our culture has decreased because of
the continued entrance of new influences. (There would be those who
would argue that Christianity itself is ultimately non-transferable to
our culture because properly understood our culture has no place
within it for religion.) We need not pursue this now but instead look
at the example of Eskimo culture in a little more detail.

It might seem that all we have been saying is that the imagery of
the Bible may not be our imagery; all the translator of the Bible has
to do is to look in the Eskimo's world for some image which will
express the lamb of God he finds in Scripture. The problem is much
deeper. I imagine, though I have never talked with an Eskimo, that
his attitude to the animal creation would be different from that of an
Israelite; to the Eskimo the animal world is much more hostile—
even his husky dogs are fierce and never become pets—than to the
Israelite; here we ourselves probably have an attitude much nearer
that of the Israelite than the Eskimo; we can understand the attitude
of the shepherd to his lambs through the kind of attitude we have to
a puppy or a kitten, though again our attitude is not entirely the
same—as we would quickly realize if someone killed our favorite
dog and served it up for dinner. For the Eskimo it is not just the
imagery in relation to sheep which is missing; the love and care of

the Israelite shepherd for his animals represents an attitude of which the Eskimo knows nothing—this is a cultural difference.

At this point we need to beware of assuming that all we are saying is that our situation is different from that of Scripture and we cannot apply Scripture directly to our situation. Cultural change is something very different from a change in situation, and it is with cultural change that we are now concerned. We shall deal later with the importance of change of situation,[3] but now let us look briefly at a mixed cultural and situational change. Most of 1 Corinthians chapters 8—10 is taken up with Paul's answer to a problem raised by the Corinthians: what is to be their attitude to food that has been sacrificed to idols. It was a genuine problem. Food left over from temple sacrifices was often on sale in the market; if a butcher slaughtered a cow he probably offered the tail, or some other not too costly part, on the altar of his favorite deity to sanctify the remainder of the carcass; it was thus difficult to purchase meat that had not in some small way been offered to an idol. In passing we should point out that becoming a vegetarian would not have been a viable solution because many other kinds of food on sale had been sacrificed. Even if it was possible it was not enough to get around the problem by being very careful over what was bought. What happened when a Christian was invited out for a meal in someone else's house? He could not be sure that what he ate had never been near an idol. Paul's answer to these problems need not delay us; it is of no importance for us; it is only an academic question—one suitable for New Testament examinations! And that is what is most significant about it—its irrelevance for the way we live our lives. But it can still be important for some Christians. There are areas of the world, e.g. Malaysia, where if a young man who lives at home is converted to Christianity, he is faced with this problem. All the food at home will have been offered to the "god" of the home; if he protests he will be told, "You either eat what is provided, or you starve." Paul's advice could be very helpful to him, but not to us because we do not face the problem. Of course, what we tend to do is to try and look for an equivalent situation and translate into that situation what Paul has been saying—and Paul's teaching here has been re-applied to all kinds of problems: drinking, gambling, etc.;

but when the translation is analyzed it is usual to find that the parallel situation is not parallel and when pushed breaks down.

We shall look at "situations" again but now we turn more directly to "culture." Our culture is, of course, not the same as any of those of the ancient world. The two with which Christianity was at first principally concerned were the Jewish and Hellenistic; if we were to include the Old Testament we would have to widen this list considerably. As we have already explained no rigid line of demarcation can be drawn between these two. Yet there was sufficient distinction between them for us to be able to say that the first cultural transformation which Christianity made (it is better to say "made" than "suffered" because it must in part have been deliberate and conscious) was that from the Judaism in which it was cradled into Gentile Hellenism, though Diaspora Judaism was a stepping stone between the two. Instead of tracing out this transformation we shall contrast our own culture with these two cultures; sometimes it differs widely from both; sometimes it differs less from one than from the other.

It is an odd thing to contemplate but the historical criticism which Christian scholars of the last two centuries adopted and developed as their principal tool (which most of them hoped would lead to a fuller understanding of Scripture by showing its background) has in fact led to our awareness of the difference between the world then and the world now. The more scholars worked at the biblical documents and the culture in which they lay, the more they became aware of the tremendous difference between their writers and ourselves, and it is a difference, not just of situation, but of culture. It is possible to draw attention to only a few of these differences. Naturally no one difference can be isolated from others and examined solely by itself; every aspect of culture runs into and merges with other aspects; thus in the few aspects which we pick it may be the same thing which is being said from different angles. On the one hand what is said may sound repetitive, and on the other, since a selection has to be made, some essential differences between our culture and those of the ancient world may not be mentioned.

1. In the ancient world there was no concept of laws of nature. We, however, assume that events in nature will continue as in the past; the sun will rise tomorrow; seed sown will in time produce plants and then

a harvest, and if the plants do not mature this is because they have been attacked by some disease or pest. Everything happens according to law; we may not be able to formulate all the laws at present, but we are confident that this will be done some day.[4] This acceptance that the laws of nature rule is an assumption in people's lives today on which they never consciously reflect. Neither did the man of biblical times who believed that all these things happened directly through the action of his God or gods. For him there were no "second causes." If it thundered this was the voice of a god:

> The voice of the LORD is upon the waters;
>   the God of glory thunders,
>   the LORD, upon many waters.
> The voice of the LORD is powerful,
>   the voice of the LORD is full of majesty.
> . . . .
> The voice of the LORD flashes forth flames of fire. (Ps.29:3–4, 7)

If today there is a famine in India reporters tell us how for a number of years the monsoon has failed, i.e., they provide a scientific explanation. In biblical times the famine would have been directly attributed to God and men would have looked to see where they had offended him. There are still some people who talk like that today; if some disaster comes to the nation they attribute it to a failure to observe the Sabbath; that most of us find this laughable shows how far our attitude has changed. Such a change necessarily affects the way we look at Scripture. It is not just that we now look on Psalm 29 as poetry which is not to be understood in a literal way; we can write it off as the imagery of the period and it does not trouble us, and it should not. But what about miracles? To think of God intervening to hold back the sun or to restore eyesight to a blind person was quite natural for someone of that time. I wrote "God intervening," but no one in the ancient world would have said that. For them God's action in staying the sun is just a part of his action in making it cross the sky from dawn to sunset; it may be exceptional and worthy of record because it only happens rarely, but it can be fitted into the frame of reference of everyday thought. Now even if we believe miracles happened we would never dream of fitting them into the frame of everyday thought; for us they are total exceptions, not just events out of the ordinary;

they are *interventions* of God. This is relevant when we try to understand for ourselves the significance of the so-called miracles, and we
shall return to their treatment later.[5] It is also related to prayer. In
prayer are we asking God to intervene? This is mentioned, not in
order to discuss it but to show that our change of culture has created
problems for us that earlier generations did not know.

2. In the ancient world crises in the order of nature had to be left
to God or the gods. If there was a famine, then, according to one's
religion, there were a number of things which might be done: prayer
could be offered for rain, or dry weather as the case might be, and
probably at the same time there could be an acknowledgment of sin
so that the god's anger would be turned away; sacrifices could be
offered to the god with the same ideas in mind or, more crudely, with
the idea of appeasing him; the witch-doctor would be approached and
his magic used (and magic was widespread in the Hellenistic world).
It is fair to say that the ancients did not just stop there; if they thought
famine was coming they could be wise enough to make preparations
to keep corn during the seven good years, but we ought to note that
it was not because scientists told them that they were entering a bad
sun-spot cycle or that there would be a drastic climatic change if
Concorde or aerosol sprays were allowed to affect ozone levels in the
stratosphere; it was because there had been a warning in a dream. We
trust present-day national leaders not to make major decisions of this
type because of their dreams! The ancients knew about moving food
from one area to another to help famine; corn could be sent from
Egypt to Palestine or relief from Antioch to Jerusalem. If we see
famine threatening areas we go much further than moving food. We
attempt to manipulate the existing natural state: we seek to get people
to use contraceptives to keep down the level of population; we instruct
them in the use of fertilizers; we breed new varieties of rice which will
give higher yields. I am not raising here the question which some ask:
Is it right to interfere with nature? Neither am I making any attempt
to answer it, but rather outlining the way in which ordinary people
react to problems: they assume there is a technological solution and
when they discover it they put it into effect. The attitude of the ancient
before creation was one of fear and reverence: the attitude of the

modern is one of manipulation;[6] there may be parts of nature which at present he cannot manipulate as he wishes, e.g., the climate, but he is certain that some day he will be able to control all of it. The size of the family to the ancient was a matter of abstinence, prayer, and magic, to the modern it is simply a pill. And with that example we can see that there is created a whole world of problems in ethical behavior which were unknown to the ancients. It is sufficient to mention one; the point at which the unborn child becomes a person is our problem because the doctor can abort safely and easily, and it is assumed that what science can do, ought to be done.

It is not science as such which has changed our culture but the technology which has grown out of science. Science discovers electricity but it is technology which creates electric power and so the capability of doing things of which the ancients never even dreamt. The artist's attitude to nature traditionally has been contemplative; the technologist's is active, he wishes to alter nature itself.

> We are all grateful for the comfort and security of life that is achieved by modern technology, and prepared to accept the claim that all these good things are the by-products of scientific research. Moreover, in the common-sense understanding of man's relations with his natural environment, and even with his fellows, "science" reigns supreme. Supernatural explanations of natural events, even of great disasters, are no longer taken seriously. The areas of ordinary life where inherited craft-wisdom is valued more highly than the judgements of scientific experts, are shrinking down to the vanishing point. This arises partly from the increasing artificiality of our material environment, and from the rapid changes in it as well as in our social environment. A sign of the triumph of "science" is the reliance on textbooks for such personal crafts as rearing children and even achieving a happy married life. This tendency is more marked in the United States than anywhere else; there the prevailing assumption is that every problem, personal and social as well as natural and technical, should be amenable to solution by the application of the appropriate science.[7]

The man of today cannot sit back and wait; he must anticipate and change.

Technology has made another change; our outlook is no longer parochial but global. We are aware of the inter-relation of the different areas of the world. We can no longer believe that what we do in our small corner has no effect elsewhere. We have thus to deal with ethical problems which did not concern the people of the Bible.

3. We have a different view of evil from the ancients. It is not that we regard different activities as evil from those the ancients did; that may be true. But for the ancient evil was supernatural; for the modern it is natural. The ancient thought of evil as coming from outside the human world: from the devil and his demons, from the stars under which he was born, from the powers and principalities which rule the universe, from luck, or rather her absence, from blind Moira ready to cut a person's life off regardless of what enjoyable things were happening to him, from his own body which was not really his true self but his prison. Now, admittedly, some of this was accepted much more wholeheartedly in the Hellenistic world than in the Jewish; it was only in the period just prior to the New Testament that Jewish thought began to give an important role to Satan as God's opponent and as origin of evil. But how many people think of evil as external in any of these ways today? We believe it is sociologically conditioned, and explain crime as the result of social, psychological, and economic deprivation. Where the ancient thought he could do nothing about evil we believe that we can change the conditions under which it flourishes and so reduce and finally eliminate it. It is true that sometimes there is still talk about the demonic in life: Nazism was described regularly as demonic; but nobody seriously thought of exorcising Hitler or the German nation; instead the more important Nazis were put on trial in courts of law as though they were wholly responsible for their actions—and despite what was often said in wartime in the pulpit about demonic evil, most people did not believe there were actual supernatural evil forces at work. It is true there may be today a recrudescence of belief in the supernatural power of evil and in the influence of the stars for good and evil: but most people who say they believe in these things do not order their lives as if they did but as if everything was explicable in human terms. Our technology itself leads us to view evil differently. If we want to view it as external then we invent men from outer space with whom we have to contend and yet whom we know are not real. Sometimes we even see evil within our own technology: we fear the nuclear holocaust we ourselves have

invented; we abhor the rat-race in which we have got ourselves involved. But all this evil is of our own creation. Finally while our
technology leads us to attack famine and disease wherever we see it,
it can also make us apathetic. Before the mass media were developed
a man saw only the evil which happened around him and about which
he could do something. Now he sees war, famine, and earthquakes
almost as they happen five thousand miles away, and feels helpless;
so he becomes indifferent and does nothing with regard to the evil that
is close at hand.

4. We have a different view of personality from the ancients, and
that in two ways. (a) When we read the Old Testament we discover
in it a much stronger sense of group personality than we possess, as
an example from one of its latest parts will show. When Daniel was
delivered from the den of lions the king punished those who had
plotted to kill him by throwing them to the lions, but he ordered that
not only the conspirators themselves should be thrown into the den
but also their wives and children; and the lions ate them all. We would
not consciously condemn the families of criminals with them, even
though we might make them suffer in other ways. This group personality of the family made much easier the acceptance of infant baptism
in the early church; much of our hesitancy about it arises just because
we think of faith as an individual matter. But group personality can
be wider than the family; it lies behind the presentation of Adam as
the originator of sin and the church as the body of Christ, not just an
organization which functions like a body, but the body of Christ. And
many scholars believe it also lies behind Paul's concept of salvation
through Christ; the benefits which men receive through his death are
theirs because of his solidarity with mankind. (b) The second way in
which earlier concepts of personality may differ from ours comes from
the other culture which we find in the New Testament—the Hellenistic. For a long time Christian thinking was dominated by the Hellenistic separation of body and soul, in which the soul was stressed as
all-important and the body downgraded as its tomb or prison. Today
we have a much more integrated view of personality, viewing the
person as a psychosomatic whole, and we are much more aware of the
inter-action of the different aspects of one person on another. This is

in part a return to more Jewish way of thinking, but since the creeds
of the church tended to be formulated in terms of a Hellenistic psychology which is no longer ours and since we tend to see the New
Testament through the eyes of the creeds this can affect the way in
which we set out a Christology.

5. This is really a summary of much that has already been mentioned but looks at it from a different angle; put briefly it is: our lives
are no longer set in a God-reference. In the ancient world the "supernatural" was a recognized part of life. God, the various gods, the stars,
were controlling factors in what went on in everyday life, and in
making plans, they had to be taken into account. When the man of
earlier days said "Aphrodite touched my heart" or "Eros shot an
arrow into my heart," Aphrodite or Eros were not metaphors, as
Cupid is for us, but real beings; indeed we seriously consider whether
love is not due to "genes" and make use of computer dating. To the
Jew the distinction between the religious and the secular sides of life
was unknown. His life was lived before God; one Law covered all of
it, relating both to what we term "civil government" as well as to the
government of the religious life. God occupies a very much smaller
place in our lives today than he did in biblical times. There is still a
national religion which functions on great occasions but not in the
things that really matter: it is improbable that any present government
would call for a day of national humiliation because of inflation. We
still recognize the existence of evil, but we no longer see it as sin,
something which is wrong in the sight of God. When small church
bodies denounce prominent people because they judge that these people have acted contrary to God's law we quietly smile. It is just
possible that we agree with the denunciation, but we would never put
it that way. It may be that in moments of terrible despair for themselves or their loved ones people pray to God, but they do not normally reckon with him as a feature of life. The dimension of God in
relation to human evil has almost completely disappeared from the
way we live. What does that mean then if we want to talk about
repentance and forgiveness? The Bible always sets them in terms of
our repentance before God and our forgiveness by him while in practice in daily life we only reckon with repentance towards other men

for the wrong we have done and we seek only their forgiveness (if we even do that!). Certainly it is true that in the ancient world there were many pagan religions in which there was little sense of sin in the terms in which the Bible depicts it, but the sense of the supernatural was still there and the belief that the supernatural could be offended by what was done. We admit the existence of "conscience" but it is no longer, as it was for earlier generations, "the voice of God."

New concepts of God are probably open to us. Some time ago a survey of religious opinion was carried out in Britain. People were asked if they believed in God; if they answered yes they were then asked: "When you think of God, do you see him as 'A Person' or 'Some kind of impersonal power'?" Less than half thought of him as a person. The same questions were later put to Anglican theological students in Papua, New Guinea. Naturally they all believed in God but they found it difficult to understand the distinction between "personal" and "impersonal"; for them all gods and spirits were "persons."[8] To most, if not all of the Bible, the concept of an "impersonal" God would have been impossible. An impersonal God will be transcendent, if he is transcendent at all, in a different way from a personal.

Some who read this may be feeling that they do not think in the ways in which people today have been described as thinking, but that they think and react in ways which lie much nearer the biblical culture or cultures. This is probably true, but no attempt has been made to describe how those who either are convinced Christians or have received some training in theology think or react; instead we have tried to understand how ordinary people live in a general kind of way in our culture. It would be surprising if members of the Christian subculture thought and reacted in exactly the same ways as others in our Western culture. Yet it is in that Western culture which we have been describing that the Bible, which came from a different culture, has to be understood, interpreted, preached.

This leads on to another difference between our world and the ancient world. Our culture is much less homogenous. Within its allowable limits there is a much greater variety of outlook and conviction. We indicate this when we speak of a "pluralist society." But even where there are no differences created by people coming from different cultures (West Indian, Puerto Rican, African, etc.) into our existing culture the variations between rural and urban, suburban and run-down inner city, "pop" and "square," mean that there are fewer common factors unifying culture than there were in an area in the ancient world. And often these variations, this fragmentation of culture leading to many sub-cultures, are found within the congregation to which one man has to preach. Consequently the transference of the meaning of Christ from Jewish and Hellenistic cultures to our culture is made even more difficult.

Further we must be careful not to confuse the message of the Bible, to use an old-fashioned term, with the culture in which that message was first expressed. At one stage there was a vogue for saying that the Bible was expressed in Jewish categories and that therefore theology ought to be expressed in these; but when these allegedly Jewish characteristics were examined they turned out to be Semitic characteristics, i.e. the culture was not Jewish alone but belonged to a much wider area. Indeed many would argue that the burden of the prophetic protest in Israel was a protest against the prevailing con-temporary Palestinian culture. And surely when Paul spoke of the cross as a stumbling-block to the Jew and as folly to the Gentile what he was doing was to criticize at a very basic level Jewish and Hellenis-tic cultures. It is important to keep this in mind, especially when we go on to consider the expression of the truth of God in our culture; if we express it in terms which can be appreciated by those who belong to our culture, this does not mean that we must make God's truth at home in our culture. As with the prophets and Paul any expression of Christ today will be an expression which will stand over against culture. In its movement into Hellenism the New Testament picked up from the mystery religions the term "regeneration" but that did not mean that it accepted the view of the mystery religions about God and man. If we express Christ today we will have to do it in the terms of our culture but that does not mean that we shall do it in such a way that we accept that culture. Christianity must always be in the prevailing culture but it is not "*of* that culture." Yet this does not mean that Christianity will be equally critical of all cultures and equally a stranger in all cultures; it will be more at home in some cultures, perhaps because through the passage of time it has succeeded in partially affecting those cultures.

More concretely, can our understanding of creation be unaffected by modern science? Can our understanding of the end of all things be unaffected by scientific views on the end of the universe? Will we replace the concept of Christ's return with an expectation that a dead star will some day crash into the earth or with the belief that a classless society represents the End? What happens when we move into the area of miracle? Will current philosophical and scientific views about the closed character of the laws of nature forbid us believing in God's intervention? Much advertising carries a blatant or implicit sexual tone; if this way of expressing ourselves has so large a place in our society ought we to express our faith in sexual terms? Before we answer no, we should remember that Scripture and the Christian mystics have regularly used sexual language. It may be possible to use sexual terms in such a way as to be understood in, and at the same time be critical of a sexually oriented culture. If we express the biblical faith in terms of today that does not necessarily mean it must be expressed within the terms of modern science, philosophy, and sociological culture and confined within the limits which they set.

If there are great differences between the world of the Bible and our world, so that the biblical imagery and conceptuality become remote from us, is it at all possible to cross this divide? Are the two areas not so far apart that there is no way from one to the other? Is there no bridge from the ancient world to our world? Of course there is. While features of our culture when set against those of the ancient world may seem so different as to suggest discontinuity we need to remember that culture is continuous. The culture in which we live is a weaving together of Greek and Jewish culture, with strands from others, and it is possible to trace the development of our culture from the cultures of ancient times and to observe the influences that have played on it and changed it. This continuity is the bridge between our world and the world of the Bible, and it is here that church history becomes relevant for us. It is not an abstract, academic subject un-related to the understanding of the precipitations of Christ in the New Testament. The tradition which flowed into and out of the New Testament writings flows onward as the history of the church. It is

a continuous succession of precipitations of which certain stand out
as landmarks. One example will suffice: Luther's precipitation within
his own experience of the New Testament teaching on justification;
this precipitation has held a dominant position within Protestantism
with the result that most Protestants tend to see Paul's teaching
through the experience of Luther. That is to say: the precipitation that
took place in Luther's experience is used in order to understand Paul.
As a result much Protestant theology has seen justification as the
attempt on man's part to put himself in the right with God, first
through his actions as Luther did through penance and good works,
and then, when he has found this a futile exercise, by the discovery
of the grace of God. Other traditions see Paul through other precipitations of the tradition. An understanding of the great precipitations
within the church can thus help us to frame our own precipitations
more precisely because these precipitations of history took place midway, as it were, in the cultural change between then and now. The
person who has been brought up in a Christian community will have
absorbed a great deal of this into his being. He belongs to a strand of
the tradition. If, however, we attempt to detach ourselves from tradition then we have a much more difficult task before us in seeking the
precipitations for our time. Often when men move away from one of
the main traditions because they may have seen with great clarity one
aspect of the precipitation for today they tend to be carried further
and further away; it is in this way that many small sects have come
into existence. Yet if it is important for each of us to realize that our
tradition is of great help to us in the formation of our precipitation
we need in this ecumenical age to remember that our tradition is not
the only tradition; there is much to learn from the precipitations that
have taken place within other traditions.

However if we are to be fair it must be acknowledged that the
Reformation does not stand midway in culture between the ancient
world and ours; it lies much nearer to the former. Though the Renais-
sance preceded the Reformation, its impact on culture was only fully
felt much later; and the Reformation itself helped to change Western
culture. The really dramatic transformation did not come until the
scientific and technological revolutions of the nineteenth and twentieth centuries. That is why those who attempt to restate theology
today in Reformation terms usually find that they have little trouble

in showing that their systems agree with biblical thought; they have much more difficulty in showing that they possess meaning in our world.

Another point may be added here to help in understanding the issue: missionaries who go to the less civilized areas, e.g., central Africa, often say that they are much nearer to the world of Scripture in those areas than in their homelands; the customs, ways of thought, cultures of primitive peoples resemble more closely what we read of in the Bible than what we are accustomed to. The idolatrous worship denounced in the Old Testament is found again in the religions of these peoples; the corporate unity of the family is as alive among them as it was in the Bible; the place of the story-teller is the same as then. Thus those who use the Scriptures in these areas can move more directly from them to actual situations in the existing culture.[9] But they do not always do it. When missionaries first went to these and other areas they took with them the understanding of Christianity which had been developed through many centuries of European culture and they demanded that their converts should see Christianity in its Western colors. So nineteen centuries of development were set between the convert and Scripture; if they had not been kept there by the missionary the convert would have got to the Scriptures more easily. Many missionaries, of course, do not behave in this kind of way today—or at least the wiser ones do not. They set out instead to make Christianity at home in the culture to which they have gone, or rather, because they can never really do this in view of their own conditioning by Western culture, they encourage the local churches to express their faith in the terms of their own culture.[10]

Up to now we have dealt mainly with the nature of the New Testament, with the culture of its time and with the culture of our time. It is necessary now to look at ourselves. Most Christians will feel that they only fit somewhat unevenly into the cultural picture of the modern world which has been sketched. But if we are going to preach what is in Scripture and apply it to our own lives, or if we are going to discuss it with others in a class or group, we need to know the culture of which, whether we agree with it or not, we are a part. Consciously or unconsciously both their lives and ours are molded by that culture.

To discuss how we come to understand the culture in which we live would lead us too far away from our main interest. No one gets to know his culture if he is completely identical with it. White people are never conscious of their whiteness and the culture which adheres to whiteness while they continue to live among other whites alone; only when they come in contact with black culture do they begin to become aware of the cultural significance of whiteness. Europeans never become conscious of European culture until they encounter a non-European culture, and the further it is removed from the European, e.g., an Indian or African culture rather than a North American, the easier it is for them to appreciate the special characteristics of their own culture. A personal reference may be excused. I have found it fascinating to observe students from Northern Ireland who have come to study in Scotland. Most of them come from Protestant homes; they make a proud boast to be British; they are certain that back home in Northern Ireland they were standing up for what is British. Gradually they change; they begin to look at what is happening in Northern Ireland from what might be described as a more detached angle, but could more properly be described as a more British angle; as this happens they realize that the British tradition was not being as faithfully copied back home as they had thought and that what they termed British was less British than they imagined. Most people are not in the position of being able to get outside their culture in order to be able to look back at it; how then can they become aware of it? There are those who make a profession of studying culture—certain brands of sociologists; their writings can be read. More importantly within every culture there are those who sense it more clearly than others: dramatists, novelists, painters. Some of them seem to be able to reflect culture and yet stand far enough away from it to be aware of its main characteristics. It is true many artists are not like this; but they are rarely those who are remembered afterwards; they are the imitators of the great artists of the last generation. At first sight there is no way of picking out from the run-of-the-mill artists those who can perform this function for us. Perhaps they are those whose work at first tends to shock us.

Indeed it has often been said about the Old Testament prophets that the true test of their genuineness was their unsettling effect on those among whom they lived; they never spoke good of society but ill. This brings us back after a great deal of wandering to something which we have largely ignored while discussing culture, viz., world-view. Each person has his own world-view; it is formed in part by the culture in which he has been brought up and in part by what he knows of other cultures and by the effect on him of others who have been aware of other cultures. No one's world-view wholly coincides with the culture in which he lives. Some people's world-view differs quite considerably. To revert to a point already made, we will be aware as we look at our culture of a certain distancing of ourselves from it. This is because our world-view does not wholly coincide with our culture. Why does it not coincide? Because, if we are Christians, we will always have been aware of one other sub-culture or group world-view, one way of thinking and reacting to situations which is not identical with that of our culture—the way of thinking and reacting which we call Christian and which we find in Scripture and the Church. The world-views of the writers of Scripture, and it is important to say "world-views," plural and not singular because of what was said about the nature of Scripture, never wholly coincided with the cultures of their time, and as we have read Scripture we have always been aware of this. Our world-views, either because they have been formed unconsciously and gradually from our earliest days or through some determined resolution to change by the world-views of Scripture, are necessarily different from those of our own culture. The significance of this difference needs to be explored a little further.

As Christians we do not go to Scripture as something utterly remote from us, belonging to a by-gone and irrecoverable age; nor do we go as those who have to understand it wholly afresh. We stand within a tradition which has been understanding Scripture through the centuries of church history. We thus have an initial understanding of it and of how it is to be understood in relation to the problems of the world in which we live. But also it is because we have an initial understanding of the world-views of Scripture that we have an initial understanding of our culture. There is no need to argue which of these came first; we probably came to them simultaneously. What must be seen is that they are interrelated. Philosophers speak in this connection of the hermeneutical circle. We come to a passage of Scripture with some awareness of its meaning and we ask it questions in the light

of our understanding; the questions are modified and reformed in the
light of what we read or of the questions Scripture puts to us and so
our understanding is deepened; this in turn modifies our questions;
and so we go on in a kind of circle. It is better to think of two circles,
or perhaps two spirals would be more correct; we ourselves form the
link between these two circles or spirals. On one side of us is Scripture
and on the other our world. We begin with an initial understanding
of each; we play one against the other and our knowledge of each is
deepened, narrowed in towards its center by our knowledge of the
other. The questions we put to Scripture come from us as members
of a culture in a particular stage of its development. Men did not start
to ask Scripture questions about slavery out of the blue but because
they saw other men being ill-treated by their owners; but they also
only saw that these men were ill-treated because from their existing
Christian experience they had some idea of what good treatment was.
Equally the questions we put to culture come to us from the Christian
world-view in which we have been brought up. It is the interplay of
Scripture and culture with our world-view which brings us to see what
Scripture means to us and the world in which we live.

There is however an added complication; it might appear that we
are assuming culture to be static; in fact it is always changing. The
understanding of culture with which we start is that of our fathers,
or of our grandfathers—and sometimes it goes much further back.
And the understanding of Scripture which is our initial understanding
is that of our fathers and of our grandfathers. We are involved then
in the first instance in refining these initial understandings but as we
do so we find that they are inapplicable because what we have to
understand, the world in which we live, has not waited until we should
fully grasp our fathers' understanding but has moved on. It is this very
flux of culture which makes inadequate the image we used of the two
spirals, for it might suggest that we could home-in on a final and
correct understanding of Scripture and our culture. This can never be
done though it is the illusion of many academics that a final and
correct understanding of some passage of Scripture or doctrine in it
can be attained; the history of the interpretation of the New Testament shows clearly that every understanding is framed within and
relative to the total culture of the time when it was evolved; hence the

frequent changes in the mood of New Testament scholarship.[11] Our understanding can never be freed from the thought world in which we live; to think otherwise is to imagine that we can disincarnate ourselves from our world. And should those who think that redemption is in some way linked to the incarnation of God, however that is explained, believe that they can free themselves when he did not?

There is another factor here; if we are Christians, our world-view is held within the community of those who have a similar world-view, that is to say, we are members of the church. One of the formative factors on our world-view as we have it at any moment is the nurture we receive in the church. If then we allow our world-view to be modified by culture do we not run the danger of getting out of line with the world-view of the church? We may, but we should remember first that the world-view of the church is not a single world-view; there are within it a number of variations; clearly there are the variations which arise out of different traditions: Anglican, Baptist, Calvinist, Catholic, Lutheran, Methodist; there are also the variations which arise within particular denominations, which we sometimes classify as liberal, conservative, radical and which cross denominational barriers. There is plenty of variety here and it is probable that as we modify our world-view we shall still find ourselves within the total area of these world-views. And we should remember, secondly, that the various world-views within the churches have already been modified by changing culture; we are not the first who have been faced with this problem. Yet there have been times when individuals have found their world-views running contrary to all that they knew of the world-views of the churches and of the existing Christian sub-cultures. World-views of churches change in the end not because of committee deliberations and decisions, but because some one person has modified his own world-view under the pressure of the Bible, or rather of that of which it is the precipitate, and the pressure of developing culture, and has then persuaded other Christians to change their world-views.

Now it may seem that instead of writing in terms of world-views it would have been proper to write instead in terms of theologies, and indeed much of what has been said could as easily have been expressed in terms of personal theologies and the various theologies of the churches. Yet the other word has been chosen deliberately because we sometimes shrink from accepting the fact that theology is in part a product of culture; it does not equal culture because it is rather the precipitation of Christ within a particular culture, thought out and unified. But theology is also somewhat narrower in field than world-view for it seems to restrict us to statements about what we would call religious matters. That this may be a wrong definition of theology is neither here nor there; it is the one with which many people operate. A world-view by definition is comprehensive. The interaction between what is precipitated in Scripture, what has nurtured me in the church, the culture around me, and me with my existing world-view will cover every aspect of life: it will be as wide flung as culture itself. But if for a moment we restrict ourselves to the term theology and its more restricted outlook then much of what has been said could be expressed by saying that all biblical interpretation is *into, through,* and *out of* a theology. Interpretation of Scripture never takes place in a vacuum but by means of a theology: and yet in the very process of passing through that theology it modifies it so that it becomes a new theology. Now it is this relation to theology that makes interpretation so difficult for us today. There were periods in the church when certain theologies dominated; theologians today find very great difficulty in systematizing their subject in such a way that there is some general agreement among them. The variety of theologies implies that there will be much less agreement over interpretation and that there will be varieties of interpretation. It is because people have different views about the way God acts, i.e., different theologies, that they take different views about miracles and so interpret them differently, or take different views about the cross and God's action in it.

Now it might seem that there was a way out of this variety of theologies by arguing that there is a biblical theology which should settle all issues; any interpretation must be in accord with biblical theology and biblical theology will itself show what theologies are possible. Against this there are two immediate objections: (1) There is no biblical theology; there are a number of theologies in the Bible; there is no New Testament theology; there are a number of New Testament theologies; this is a corollary to what was said about precipitations. (2) Even if there were only one theology in the Bible it would still have to be expressed in our culture in order to check whether a theology of our culture was in accord with it. If by academic work it was possible to unearth the biblical theology and express it in its own terms and supposing we could understand it if we did it in that way, it would still not be possible to check a theology which had emerged in a culture without some means of crossing cultures. That would require either the ability to express the biblical theology in our culture or the theology arising in our culture in terms drawn from the Bible. The problem resembles an attempt to measure a piece of wood for a shelf given the shelf size in metric measure when we only have a ruler which is marked in feet and inches and we do not know the conversion factor between the two scales of measurement.

But ought we not to be content with a biblical theology expressed in its own terms? In John's Gospel we find the teaching of Jesus transmuted into new terms; it is regularly pointed out that John uses "life, eternal life" where Jesus himself used "kingdom of God." John was aware that he was transmuting the message and significance of Jesus and he gives a justification for it: the Holy Spirit will lead Christ's followers into truth; he is the Spirit of truth who bears witness about Jesus and guides into all the truth (John 14:26; 15:26; 16:13,14). The Spirit is not dead; he still guides and leads us to new understandings of Jesus in our terms within our culture. We cannot believe that the Spirit's work in leading men into truth ceased with the writing of the New Testament or with the primitive church. It is in the confidence that he still leads that we must go about our task of interpreting.

3
scRiptuRe in
ouR woRld

We have outlined a view of Scripture and of suggested differences between the world of Scripture and our world. How then is Scripture to be understood in our world? The chaplain of a boys' school once gave a talk to his students which he illustrated by showing them a hammer, a saw, and other tools. Afterwards he met one of the mothers, and she said to him, "Jimmy came home and told us about your talk and now he realizes that Jesus was a real man." The next day he met another of the mothers and she said "Billy came home and told us about your talk. Why don't you stick to the Bible and teach the boys what's in it?" Those are two very different attitudes to the way in which we understand Scripture, express our understanding and relate it to our world. For the moment it is pointless to argue which of them is correct; it is enough to say that there is no simple way of decoding the message (this is too verbal a term; it is not a set of words but Christ who is the center of Scripture) of Scripture from the words in which it lies at present and then of encoding it in the world of today.

Before we discuss some of the devices or mechanisms which are used to "decode" Scripture, it is important to realize that we are not attempting to understand and use the writings of those who are wholly foreign to us because they either lived so long ago or their culture and situations were so different. With them we share an understanding of God and ourselves which we do not necessarily share with all other people of that age or even of our own. We come to their writings because we have an experience which is basically the same as theirs—an experience of God's mercy in Jesus Christ. By this we are enabled to interpret them. Our common understanding helps to bridge the gap between them and their writings and ourselves and our world. We do not go with open and neutral minds to their writings; we go as possessors of an experience which we wish to deepen so that it permeates all our living, and as those who have some initial sympathy with what we interpret.

The remoteness of the words, however, may at times compel us to use some device or trick in order to unlock the meaning they contain. Such techniques have been in use from the beginning to make Scripture relevant. We are the more likely to use one of these techniques if we heed the advice of many homileticians and first find a text before thinking of what we shall say. Starting in this way we may look on Scripture as a deep freeze. When we need a sermon we go and bring out a text and after a suitable period of defrosting and cooking our meal is ready. We go on now to examine some of these techniques.

(1) There are those who would say that Scripture is to be taken just as it stands, that indeed we have been creating a problem where no real problem exists; the truth that is in Scripture is to be believed in the way it is stated and the commands that it contains are to be obeyed in the way that they are set down. Those who argue in this way would not claim that Scripture is to be understood in the language of the King James Version; they would agree that it is to be put in modern language so that it may be understood more easily, and its plain meaning become more clearly visible. The Reformers laid great stress on the plain meaning of Scripture, believed that it could be easily ascertained, and when ascertained that it became the operative. All that is needed is to transfer it with a few simple adaptations to our situation. We might call this the method of *direct transference*. Many, but by no means all, in the neo-pentecostalist movement work from this kind of understanding of Scripture. Because they read about speaking in tongues and the healing of the sick in the New Testament and because gifts for these activities are promised they therefore conclude that they themselves ought to display these gifts in their lives; in like manner, classical Reformation teaching expected that the Church organization which it discovered in the Pastoral Epistles should be the organization which would always exist within the

Church, i.e., the organization of the Church today should be the organization which we find in the Church of the New Testament. It should be transferred directly to our situation.

Quite clearly certain parts of Scripture can be taken more or less at their face value and applied to us. No one who is a Christian would dispute that God is love (1 John 4:8), or would think that he was not still under the command "You shall love your neighbor as yourself." It is when we move from these simpler statements that difficulties begin. But they are present even in such simple statements. Jesus taught that God is our Father, and this looks straightforward. But what we mean by father today may not be identical with what a first century Jew conceived when the word father was used by him or to him. The culture in which a word is used gives it a nuance all of its own. We can compare the different position of the father in the family in Victorian times and now. If we say "God is Father" do we mean the father of the Victorian era or the father of our own period or some other type of father? A concept can also be affected by the personal situation of a hearer or reader; someone who comes from a broken family in which the father has been the guilty party will have a different conception of fatherhood from someone who has been brought up in a good family; the image of "father" possessed in later life by a child who was battered by his or her father will hardly be that of the Gospels. When we read the passage about Jesus taking the children to his heart and blessing them (Mark 10:13–16) we normally impose upon our understanding of this passage the concept of childhood which belongs to our culture; our culture is child-centered and we idealize children, but in the ancient world it was the mature adult who was idealized. So, because of our concept of childhood, we attribute various ideas of innocence, gentleness, wonder, or trust to the children of the story; but it is probable that the true understanding of this story with its lesson, "Whoever does not receive the Kingdom of God like a child shall not enter it," means that the person who does not consider himself as unimportant as a child was in the ancient world will not enter the Kingdom. The same difficulty can arise when we move to the area of personal griefs and sorrows. Passages from the Psalms are often used in such circumstances; the original readers of the Psalms stood in a covenant relation with God which can hardly be re-created today. There is a difficulty here which is seen when a wise pastor offers a different kind of consolation to a member of the Christian community than that which he offers to one who does not belong. We cannot therefore simply transfer a passage of consolation from Scripture to a modern situation. The way in which grief is expressed has changed vastly and is continuing to change: in large part this is due to changes in family solidarity.[1] The traditional wild grief of an Irish "keening" bears no resemblance to that of an American upper middle-class family; the first is much closer to that of the ancient Jewish and Christian world. Scripture knows nothing about the helpful use of tranquilizers as an adjunct to the pastor's comfort!

There is no need to criticize in detail this method of interpreting the New Testament for many of the criticisms made of other modes of interpretation apply in an even stronger way to direct transference; it will suffice to indicate briefly some of its weak points. (a) Situations are never the same.[2] (b) Concepts change their meanings; we have seen how "father" and "child" have changed because culture has changed. (c) There may be no equivalent concept: Eskimos lack a concept into which they can translate the biblical concept of "sheep" and "shepherd." (d) Large areas of life as it is experienced today will be left untouched if we confine ourselves to what is explicitly mentioned in Scripture; Jesus moved in a simple village society and the problems which he encountered were those of that society; they were problems in which one person came face to face with another. Many of our problems are much more complex. We run little danger of being hit on the cheek by one of our fellows, but what happens if some group of workers makes huge wage demands for itself and achieves those demands so that the standard of living of other sectors of the community is affected? Those who adopt the view of interpreting Scripture which is being considered often find themselves adopting simplistic solutions to political problems; sometimes they become pacifists because Jesus said we should love our enemies; sometimes they say that all political and social problems would be solved if everyone was converted, and leaving aside the problems they attempt to convert everyone. (e) On this theory of interpretation how do we understand those portions of Scripture which clash with one another, or those portions with which we do not agree?

The work of academic New Testament scholars has often tended to lead its hearers to the method of "direct transference." The academic goal[3] has been to explain the text in its own terms, to let its meaning appear in its own situation, and because New Testament commentators have usually stopped there they have left the impression that this was all that needed to be done. This may be satisfactory in the classroom—whether it can actually be achieved is another matter—but it is unsatisfactory in the pulpit or when anyone meditates on the meaning of Scripture so that he may mature. There is a meaning "now" to which the historical-critical method is a stage on the way, but of which it is not the full destination. It is because academics stop where they do that they run the danger of being accused of irrelevance and students wish the courses revised. Once the meaning "then" has been explained the impression must not be left that that meaning is the meaning "now," even if no attempt is actually made to discover the meaning "now."

(2) One way of avoiding some of the difficulties to which brief allusion has just been made in regard to the parts of Scripture which clash with one another or appear irrelevant to our situation is *allegorization*. This method of interpreting literature was widespread in the ancient world. There were those who, not wishing to abandon all connection with the ancient myths of the gods, took these legends and allegorized them so that philosophical truth could be derived from them. Philo, the Alexandrian Jew, used the method extensively in relation to the Old Testament. He even gave rules about where it should be used: the literal sense is inadmissible where the text says something unworthy of God, e.g., uses an anthropomorphism, or involves Scripture in contradictions (Genesis 4:17: there are not yet enough people for a city to be built by Cain, where did he get his wife?), or contains something which is manifestly allegorical, e.g., the speaking serpent (Genesis 3). The early Christians took over this method from their contemporaries. We find Origen utilizing it extensively. Where he finds contradictions in the Scriptures he assumes that we ought to look for a spiritual or allegorical meaning. Thus when he deals with the cleansing of the temple which in John appears at the beginning of Jesus' ministry and in the Synoptic Gospels at the end

he regards this as an opportunity to allegorize. In John he likens the temple to man's soul, skilled in reason and higher than the body; Jesus cleanses the soul of those things which are unworthy of it; the ox is symbolic of earthly things, the sheep of senseless and brutal things because it is more servile than most of the creatures without reason, the dove of empty and unstable thoughts, the coins of the money changers of things that are thought good but are not. And he comments

> If any one objects to this interpretation of the passage and says that it is only pure animals that are mentioned in it, we must say that the passage would otherwise have an unlikely air.[4]

There are difficulties also about the entry into Jerusalem: how many animals were there? Mark supposes one, Matthew supposes two; this suggests we ought to allegorize.

> Now Jesus is the word of God which goes into the soul that is called Jerusalem, riding on the ass freed by the disciples from its bonds. That is to say, on the simple lauguage of the Old Testament, interpreted by the two disciples who loose it. . . . But He also rides on the young colt, the New Testament; for in both alike we find the word of truth which purifies and drives away all those thoughts in us which incline to selling and buying.[5]

Allegorization becomes a temptation to those who believe that every Christian truth ought to be biblical and to be stated explicitly in Scripture. So the Old Testament is allegorized in order to discover within it the doctrine of the Trinity. The syllogism runs: the Old Testament must be used; Christ is the center of Christian faith; therefore Christ must be found everywhere in the Old Testament in his relation to the Father and the Spirit. The conclusion does not follow. Allegorization was used to such excess in earlier periods of the church that principles had to be laid down to control it and indicate when it could be appropriately employed. It was held that it could be used so long as the interpretation which was derived from it was in accord with the rule of faith, i.e., with Christian doctrine generally; allegorization should not be used to discover new doctrines, but only to verify or illustrate known doctrines; and it must not conflict with the plain meaning.

At its simplest, allegorization takes a piece of literature and makes the people or objects in the text have some symbolic meaning. The new meaning will usually bear some relation to the whole body of literature to which the text belongs, which means that in the case of Christian allegorization it will be in accord with the rule of faith, but it need have no actual connection with the content of the passage which is being allegorized. It was condemned by the Reformers yet it continues to be used by many in their tradition who believe they ought to preach from every portion of Scripture, and since some sections are so difficult there is nothing for them to do but to allegorize in order to derive some meaning. But why did the Reformers reject allegorization? And why should it be rejected today? We may of course accept their insight and yet have other or additional reasons.

(a) It is to be rejected because given sufficient ingenuity it is possible to derive practically any teaching from any chosen passage. A slight acquaintance with those who allegorize will quickly show that they tend to discover the same lesson in almost every passage of Scripture. Evangelists making use of the Old Testament for evangelical purposes invariably discover the same teaching about the death of Jesus therein. A person finds whatever he is interested in. This, by the way, brings to light another aspect of interpretation: we can call it "interest." Our prevailing "interest" will lead us either to those passages in which that interest is found or will help us to see it as the principal teaching of passages in which it is only a minor element. Interest tends to control us unconsciously. Thus the liturgiologist is always discovering references to worship; the evangelistic, to individual conversion; the person interested in the church, to corporate life; the rigorous Calvinist, to predestination. When we come to a passage of Scripture we always have within our minds certain questions and certain ways of looking at Christianity, and we tend to ask the questions which help us to understand Christianity from our angle. This is a natural phenomenon, and it is one of which we should be aware; if we always discover the same element in different passages our total understanding of our faith will not be widened and if we are preachers we shall bore the congregations which we address.

(b) Allegorization takes us away from the plain meaning of Scripture on which the Reformers insisted. If we find difficulties with the literal meaning we do not need to allegorize today for we can have recourse to the historical-critical method; it shows us how such puzzling difficulties as that of Cain's wife arose, and what such passages meant at the time they were written; we need no longer be worried because there was no woman for Cain to marry.

(c) If allegorization is to be controlled by what we know to be Christian doctrine from other parts of Scripture, as its wiser users have always decreed, then why bother to find in a particular passage what we know to exist already in some other passage? Why not go straight to this other passage and use the truth as found in it, where it is the plain meaning. And if we wish to use it to illustrate a Christian doctrine not in Scripture, why not simply use the doctrine, and eliminate the Scriptural reference? A later crystallization may be true without its truth depending directly on actual texts.

(d) It is possible to obtain exactly the same results by allegorizing passages outside Scripture. One of Aesop's fables runs as follows:

> A crow sat in a tree holding in his beak a piece of meat that he had stolen. A fox which saw him determined to get the meat. It stood under the tree and began to tell the crow what a beautiful big bird he was. He ought to be king of all the birds, the fox said; and he would undoubtedly have been made king, if only he had a voice as well. The crow was so anxious to prove that he *had* a voice, that he dropped the meat and croaked for all he was worth. Up ran the fox, snapped up the meat, and said to him: "If you added brains to all your other qualifications, you would make an ideal king."[6]

Here the piece of meat is the Word of God, the fox is the devil and the crow is the Christian; when the Christian thinks too highly of himself he loses God's Word. The essential error of allegorization must now be clear; it does not recognize the real meaning of Scripture and in effect denies the position it should occupy for the Christian since it treats Scripture as words that can be played around with and not in any way as a record of God's activity.

(e) Finally, if my understanding of Scripture is correct, allegorization has no place, for Scripture can only be interpreted in the light of the situation, culture, and world-view which led to the birth of each part of it. It is never just words but always words belonging to a context; allegorization by its very nature pays no heed to the context.

(3) Associated with allegorization as a method of interpretation is *spiritualization.* Blindness signifies the closed mind, and so the giving of sight to the blind is understood spiritually as the opening of the mind to God. Leprosy signifies sin, and so cleansing from leprosy is understood spiritually as cleansing from sin. Storm signifies trial and persecution, and so Jesus' quelling of the storm indicates spiritually the preservation of the Church in peril and persecution. Notice that all these three examples have been drawn from Scripture. The method is widely used in the Gospels in relation to the great works of Jesus, and it is often the way in which it is advocated that the miracles should be understood. Many of the attempts to show their relevance to our lives spiritualize them. The method is useful because it appears to permit the use of the miracles as passages still suitable for interpretation, though difficulties may exist in many minds whether they actually happened as recorded. Within the Gospels themselves the miracles are already spiritualized, rather than allegorized. Spiritualization as a method of interpretation is clearly not restricted to the miracles; the exodus of the Old Testament is spiritualized in the New Testament and made to signify the redemption that is in Christ; the process of spiritualizing it had already begun in the Old Testament.

Can spiritualization as a method be defended? Before we answer this we have to look briefly at the way in which miracles may be used. (a) They may be used to prove that Jesus is God. Many commentators on Mark believe that in the tradition before it came to Mark there was a chain of miracle stories which testified to Jesus' divinity; Mark took this chain and instead of leaving this emphasis he used the miracles to produce the kind of meaning which is developed through spiritualization and of which we have just given examples. (b) They may be used to prove that something new has happened with Jesus; if he exorcises, then the Kingdom of God has come (Luke 11:20). (c) They may be spiritualized. (d) They may be allegorized. There is no need to illustrate this in detail since we have already discussed allegorization. Origen allegorizes the feeding of the five thousand: Jesus ordered the people to sit on the grass; all flesh is grass; by sitting on the grass we are to understand the holding of the flesh in submission.[7] (e) They may be used to show the compassion of Jesus; wherever he encounters sickness and the sick person seeks healing from him, he shows his compassion in healing. (f) They may be used to teach Christians how to heal; after Jesus had cured the epileptic boy whom his disciples had failed to heal, he told them that such healings could only be effected through prayer (Mark 9:14–29); the purpose of this account in the Gospel is instructional, so that believers would know how to do the same. (g) They may be used to demonstrate the laws of modern psychology; when Jesus heals the paralytic of Mark 2:1–12 he first forgives his sin; sickness and sin may be linked; sickness may be psychosomatic. Of these methods of interpretation (a) is not much used in Scripture; indeed it can be argued that it is rejected (cf. Mark 8:11–13 where Jesus refused to perform a miracle in order to convince the Pharisees); the ancient world was far more accustomed to the miraculous than we are and was much less likely to be impressed by the mighty deeds of Jesus. We have already argued that (d) is an illegitimate method of interpretation. The illustration given in (g) is probably true; yet all it does is to help us to understand the miracle rather than supply us with its interpretation. (b), (c), (e) and (f) are all in Scripture. (e) appeals to those who wish to present the love of Jesus for men; (f) appeals to those who argue that spiritual healing should be practiced by the Church today. (c) appeals most of all to those who have to preach about miracles. (b) has logical difficulties for there were other successful exorcists as well as Jesus in the ancient world.

We may defend spiritualization as a method in relation to the miracles, not merely because it appears within Scripture, but because just like the Gospel writers we believe Christ opens men's minds, forgives their sins, and saves the church in times of trial. But a difficulty is bound to be raised sooner or later; if someone doubts whether Christ did still the storm at sea, can he then deduce that he will preserve the church in time of peril? The belief that Christ quells the storms that surround the church and preserves it do not in the final issue derive from the miracle; we already believe this to be true on other grounds; we then read it into the miracle and the miracle becomes an illustration of a truth which is believed on other grounds. Because we believe that sins are forgiven through Christ we read this into the story of the healing of the leper and do not ultimately derive it from the healing. Because we believe that Christ opens the minds of men to understand truth we read this into his opening of the eyes of the blind, but we do not derive it from the stories of the healing of the blind. If we have a skeptical congregation, and many Christians are far more skeptical than preachers believe, or if we ourselves are skeptical in relation to the miracles, we may find that this method of interpretation is one which it is better not to use, though the spiritualizations to which it leads are themselves true.

Of the three examples of spiritualization offered, doubts may quickly appear about two; the stilling of the storm and the healing of the leper. Has not too much been read into Scripture on these points? Behind this doubt lies one of the dangers in the use of spiritualization. Unless the image which is essential to the spiritualization is a living image both in the culture of the biblical world and in our culture we cannot use it for this purpose. Since we still use the metaphor of blindness to indicate intellectual or spiritual blindness, we can easily accept a spiritualization of the miracles of the healing of the blind in the Gospels. When, however, we come to an event like the stilling of the storm it has to be explained that this is meant to represent the quietening of the storms which surround the church; it is not directly appreciated. It may be useful to do this in order to explain why such a story is in the Gospels, but the spiritual truth does not immediately leap to mind; it might well be easier to convince others of the spiritual truth by starting from another passage of Scripture. The movement from the healing of leprosy to the forgiveness of sins will also seem artificial except to those who have been brought up in a strong biblical tradition. Once spiritualization becomes artificial it comes dangerously near to passing into allegorization.

It may also be difficult to control the technique. Is it to be restricted to those occasions where it is present in Scripture, or may incidents be taken and spiritualized in ways which are not found in Scripture? In Mark 2:1–12 we have the story of a paralytic whom Jesus healed.[8] Is it permissible to spiritualize this and speak of a paralysis of the mind or conscience from which Jesus delivers? There is no doubt that there are almost paralyzed consciences and minds dead to spiritual truth and there is no doubt that Jesus can awaken them, but is Mark 2:1–12 the section of Scripture from which it is right to begin to talk about them? Does not such an approach deny the contextual nature of Scripture? We are also faced with a problem to which reference was made earlier; as the stories of Jesus were passed on in the early Church they were changed. It is difficult to believe that Jesus healed the blind in order to teach men spiritual lessons; these stories may have become acted parables in the eyes of the early Church, but did not Jesus heal the sick because he saw their need? The early Christians read new meaning into this. Are we to go on reading in new meaning? Are we only to accept the new meaning read in by the church? Or should we prefer the meaning that seems to have lain in the event for Jesus himself? The New Testament's use of spiritualization shows us how the early church thought but will the method stand up to the logical criteria we apply to arguments today?

Looking back over the method of spiritualization, it must be said firmly that the method can only be illustrative, and cannot be used to prove doctrine. We cannot prove that Jesus brings understanding to our minds because he opens the eyes of the blind; that is to move from the lesser to the greater. Furthermore, we should note that it is only possible to draw general illustrations, or lessons, through spiritualization. The very method isolates the particular incident from its original situation. While it allows us to say that Jesus gives sight it does not allow us to understand in any way the content of the sight which Jesus gives to men's minds and so does not bring us any further into the understanding of the truth that is Jesus. If then we use this method, we must use it with great care and with a proper understanding of its limitations.

(4) Since the situational nature of Scripture has been stressed, it might seem logical to approach our understanding of Scripture through situations. There are two different ways in which this could be done, either beginning with a situation in Scripture, then looking to see what situation in our life corresponds to this and relating the two, or beginning with a situation in our life, then looking for a situation in Scripture which seems to correspond to it and relating the two. While it is obvious that we may not always be able to find exact parallels between the situations of Scripture and the situations of our lives, there is no doubt that there are some situations which are closely parallel. We can term this method of interpretation *parallelism*. We

are still human beings, the same kind of human beings that existed in the days of the Bible; the same God redeems us who redeemed the disciples of Jesus. In that general sense our situation is exactly the same as that of the original believers: we stand in need of God's grace as much as they did and God is still as ready to be gracious now as he was then. Much Scripture has no precise situational orientation. When we look in the Pauline letters at some of the lists of moral duties (these lists were often drawn from contemporary ethical instruction), we find little that is specifically directed to the situation of the particular church to which Paul is writing. When Paul, or whoever wrote Ephesians, says "Be ye angry, and sin not; let not the sun go down upon your wrath," (Eph. 4:26 K.J.V.) this is as relevant today to a husband who has been angry with his wife because she has burnt his dinner as it was in Paul's day; and it is equally relevant to a politician who has been embittered by some remark of an opponent; should he allow himself to be overcome by anger, his ability to make a sound judgment will be seriously impaired. Reinhold Niebuhr has a sermon in which he transfers this very text to the relationships of nations;[9] it is an excellent example of how such a movement from the individualistic to the social sphere can be carried through.

Equally the call of Scripture to men to repent could be said to be as valid today as it was in the time of Jesus. And yet even that must be qualified: Scripture calls men to repent from sin, but there are many today who do not recognize the existence of sin; they acknowledge that men make mistakes and by their activities injure others, but do not regard these as sins, that is offenses against God, for God does not exist or exists in such an impersonal way that man's situations do not impinge on him. Almost all the ancient world was unanimous in agreeing that it was possible to offend the supernatural powers ruling the universe; a great many people today would not agree. But even if the man of today admits that sin in the biblical sense exists, yet the sins from which he needs to repent may be different sins from those of the first century. Repentance from sin is a theological idea, but actual repentance is always from sins, from particular sins. Thus there are elements both of situation and of culture in the call to repent.

In Romans 5:12–21 Paul sets down a contrast between Christ and Adam and implies that because we are descended from Adam we shall

all die and do all sin. Here is a universal human situation. But can we take this as true in the same way as Paul did? We believe neither that Adam ever existed nor that we are physically descended from any first human pair. It can possibly be argued that Paul's belief about how men are related to Adam is not entirely one of physical descent but depends in part upon his belief in the solidarity of mankind, men forming the corporate personality of Adam. That, however, does not really help, for we do not normally think in terms of corporate personality in our culture. Is this part of Romans then to be discarded, or can we still make something of it, even if not in quite the same way as Paul? If we look at our society we see that we are sociologically conditioned to the way in which we live by those among whom we live; we tend to repeat their faults and their good points; this is particularly true of the families in which we have been brought up; the virtues and failings of parents often repeat themselves in the children. From the society in which we are brought up we inherit its prevailing vices and virtues, and by the example of the people around us we are led into both evil and good. It was inevitable that if Paul was to express this he should express it in terms of Adam. But we do not need to express it in that way. Indeed it is important that we should not express it in that way; too often when a preacher talks about Adam, using him as a theological symbol, his hearers think he really does believe in Adam's historical existence and write the preacher off as irrelevant. Furthermore, while Adam is normally used to explain sin, it is also important to see that it is not only sins and vices which are inherited from society but also virtues and good qualities. This can be taken a little further because for Christians one important element in the environment to which they belong is the Christian community of which they are members; it should make the influence towards virtue in them a stronger influence than would be found in the life of non-Christians.

If then there are many passages in Scripture which by reason of their content are general in nature or lack any situational orientation, a large part of the material is related to particular situations. 1 Corinthians provides an example. In it Paul discusses a number of themes which he had been informed were troubling the Corinthians. There was a tendency to adhere to certain church leaders and to express loyalty to Christ through these leaders, Paul, Peter, Apollos. Out of this divided nature of the Corinthian community Paul has certain things to say about spiritual understanding and these may still be relevant today. He goes on after this to deal with a case of incest, hardly one of the sins common in Christian congregations today. After that he deals with those Christians who having fallen out with one another over some matter go to law to settle their differences. Clearly even today church members may find themselves at law one against another; but the structure of society and the relationships of Christians within it are now so much more complex that it is not easy to say how Paul's advice ought to be followed in respect of settling disputes. In the complexities of modern society few church sessions, boards of deacons, or executive boards would wish to act as judges in a case in which there had been a breach of contract and in which the managing directors of the two firms concerned were members of the Christian community. Paul deals next with fornication and with Christians who believed that intercourse with prostitutes was irrelevant to their Christian faith. While instances of such behavior still exist, the modern believer who fell into this would have a bad conscience. On the other hand, the Corinthian Christian would have argued that the soul alone was important and if it was saved the use of the body in this way would hardly matter. Paul moves on naturally from that to the relation of man and woman in marriage, and here he does touch on issues which are still very central even in the most moral of congregations; yet much of his discussion is governed by a belief that the world is going to end shortly and that, therefore, it is better for the Christian not to marry. The time is short and there are many to be saved, therefore let the Christian attend to his main task and not be diverted by marriage. Because we do not feel the eschatological pressure in the way that Paul did, we evaluate marriage differently. From this he goes on to write about food which had been sacrificed to idols; this hardly applies in our situation.[10] There follows a long section on worship touching on a number of subjects. Whether women should wear hats in church is a question which hardly excites us today, and we are even less likely to be excited by the reasons Paul gives for his decision. In Corinth the conduct of the Eucharist had become scandalous: the community had divided into groups and these groups ate separately; the rich got drunk, the poor were hungry; our failures in our conduct in relation to the Eucharist are quite different. The last subject relating to worship with which Paul deals is "spiritual gifts," with particular reference to speaking in tongues. Here at least we have something which is relevant to the life of the church today, and the advice which Paul gives still forms the basis of the advice issued by most church councils to their members in relation to glossolalia.[11] But there is a fresh aspect which emerges here and should be noted, for it is of importance to the discussion as a whole: our situation can never be precisely the same as that of the situation of the first Christians in one crucial respect; part of our situation is our knowledge of Scripture; it can be argued that if we did not have the record of glossolalia in Scripture, glossolalia would not be found in the Church today; 1 Corinthians is itself a creative factor in our situation as it was not in Corinth in the period before Paul wrote it. The last subject to which Paul turns in his letter is that of the resurrection; will the dead be raised, and if they are raised, what will they be like? His discussion turns upon the meaning for him of the word "body." Unfortunately our English usage of this word is far from identical with Paul's; here we come on one of those cultural differences to which we have already pointed; the Semitic conception of personality was of a person as a whole; we tend to distinguish, to put it somewhat loosely, between the soul and the body. It is changes like these which make the transfer from a situation in the ancient world to a situation today so exceedingly difficult.

A second illustration can be drawn from the "social codes" which are found in several of the New Testament letters.[12] These codes, ultimately derived through Judaism from the Hellenistic world, deal with the duties of people in their social relationships, husbands and wives, parents and children, slaves and masters. We shall look only at the last of these: the slave-master relationship. Although many translations use the word "servant" in the passages which deal with this, what is really in mind is the relative position of the slave and his master and the translations "cheat" by altering subtly the meaning of the word. They do this perhaps because there is no parallel to slavery in modern life in Western Europe or North America and they wish to create one. The teaching in 1 Peter 2:18–25 is particularly difficult, for it treats only of the duty of the slave to the master and his duty is said to be that of absolute submission; whatever his master orders him to do he must do, and if he is punished by his master he must bear that punishment patiently as Christ bore his punishment. The institution of slavery is accepted, and there is no hint of condemnation. No duties are laid on masters. On the face of it it looks as if we should set aside this piece of Scripture as wholly irrelevant to our situation, yet when we examine it more closely we can see in it an underlying truth which has some relevance to us. When we compare the biblical social codes with those of the Hellenistic world, we discover that only in the former is there a section dealing with slaves. In the Hellenistic world the slave had an uncertain position; he was a possession of his master, a tool rather than a person; when social codes were compiled they were compiled for the use of free men and not intended for the use of slaves. But the Christian finding the slave in his community of believers accepted the fact that he was as much a moral person as the free man and like him had responsibilities towards God and his fellows. Thus moral duties could be set before him. For the first time the slave is fully accepted as a person and once this position has been adopted it is only a matter of time until he was freed from his serfdom (admittedly it turned out to be a very long time). In this section then we discern a realization that all men are men and are never to be dismissed as of some lesser status. We still have a habit of reducing some of them to non-persons (note the way we refer to them as "nigger," "boy," etc.).

Before we go on to look at the problem from the other side, i.e., commencing with our situation and linking it to a parallel biblical situation, a particular type of parallelism needs to be mentioned: historicizing exegesis. Some of the biblical commentaries found at Qumran practice this method; references to events and people contemporary with the biblical author are applied to the period of the commentator. In our day stories from the history of ancient Israel are taken to have a message for what is happening to us. This takes place easily in time of war or conditions of national stress or jubilation. The material has always to be carefully selected or the wrong lesson might be deduced. There are times in the Old Testament when the Southern Kingdom of Judah is commended while the Northern Kingdom of

Israel is rebuked, but preachers at Protestant services and demonstrations in Northern Ireland never seem to use these passages.[13] Those who practice historicizing exegesis usually know the answer they want and pick a passage which will provide it! The actual parallel is nearly always superficial or very general and but for the ingenuity of the preacher would never be noticed. The method normally fails as genuine exegesis because it ignores the full contextual nature of the original event.

So far we have looked at the situations of the biblical world; it is now important that we look at the situations of our own; clearly there are certain situations which are the same and we have already examined some of them. Equally clearly there are situations to which it is almost impossible to discover a parallel in the Bible. Let us look at some of these:

(a) A husband and wife through a contraceptive failure have a child on the way. Shall the woman have an abortion? Abortions admittedly took place in the ancient world, but they were hazardous and only to be attempted as a last resort. Today they can be carried through easily and safely. A new situation has been created for us by the advance of medical science. But it is not only the situation which is new, the culture has also changed. Most people believe that they ought to do whatever science or technology shows can be done. The basic question of the permissibility of an abortion is related not only to social conditions (will the extra child over-burden the family? add an unnecessary addition to the world's population?, etc.) but to the point at which true life is supposed to begin—at conception, at birth, or at some point in between. There is a similarity in this problem to another which is now appearing more regularly: is life to be terminated when the person has become a vegetable and there is no more hope of recovery? We have little compunction in putting down an animal when we see it suffer and know it has no hope of survival. But when do we pull the plug in the case of a person? When, in fact, does the person cease to be a person? There does not appear to be any clear parallel situation in Scripture which may be used as a guide.

(b) Apart from a lucky few human life in the ancient world was dominated entirely by work; the period of the working day and the period of being awake coincided; all man's time was given to sustaining himself and his family by his labor. Planned leisure was utterly unknown. There were "holy days" but their primary purpose was not recreation, though in fact they often gave an opportunity for it. That, however, was incidental. If an Israelite had been asked why he kept the Sabbath he would never have answered, "It is good to take a break once a week to refresh oneself for the week ahead," which is the answer many Christian apologists make today in respect of Sunday. Holidays, as distinct from "holy days," did not exist. Those therefore in the ancient world who took time out from the general full-time activity of work were regularly rebuked by the moralists; they were, in effect, causing others to work harder; if they did not do so there would not be enough food and people would starve. If man today in Western civilization were to spend all his time in work in that way there would be serious economic problems through over-production. The Protestant work ethic, which is associated, probably wrongly, with Calvinists, is not out of harmony with the general biblical pattern. This ethic appeared in a period when, as in biblical times, everyone had to work all the time if the level of society and civilization was to be maintained. We live in a different culture; this difference has regularly produced an internal stress in us with a feeling that we are failing unless we can justify what we are doing in terms of activity. Thus the regular embarrassment of the church in dealing with the "problem" (what a thing to call it!) of leisure. Each of us is given so many weeks' holiday in the year; we have to take them; how shall we spend them? Is it proper to relax and do nothing? Should our leisure activities be directed to the building up of our bodies in health, or the feeding of our minds with good literature and music? Should we spend our time in going to conferences in order to deepen our Christian faith? The very shape of these questions arises out of our traditional Protestant work ethic, and there is nothing in Scripture which can really be of direct help in solving them because the work ethic lay very near to the world of Scripture and is economically unacceptable today.

(c) The previous illustrations have had one thing in common; only a limited number of people are involved. In that they resemble the ethical problems which the New Testament treats. The problems we go on to deal with add a fresh complication; large numbers of people are involved in the effects of whatever action is taken.

A man belongs to a labor union; shall he vote for or take part in a strike for higher pay? There are many things to be considered; will the strike be successful or will the employees be forced back to work under worse terms because the management has greater resources than the strikers have for a prolonged period of inactivity? Will their claim for higher pay adversely affect the national economy so that in the end they will be worse off than they were at the beginning? If they do not strike will they be worse off because others who have gone on strike have managed to advance their relative position? The complexity of the situation is created by modern social and industrial conditions in which the personal problem cannot be isolated from the problem of the nation and the world.

(d) Should we travel to work by car or public transportation? If we go by car, we shall be there faster, perhaps have more time to work, and be home sooner. We shall have more time for the family, our marriage, and our home responsibilities. If we go by bus or train, we preserve the atmosphere from further pollution and we conserve the limited fuel resources of the world for our descendants.

(e) Shall we eat the eggs or the meat which is produced when animals are fed and restricted in near prison cell confinement? If we do not accept such food into our lives, will our choice of food not be more limited, and may we not have to pay more for what we do buy with the result that we have less money to give to good causes? If we do eat such food, are we not inflicting unnecessary and unnatural cruelty on animals?

To summarize, certainly there are general situations which are the same for us as for the biblical writers. Many issues in personal ethics, where one person is concerned with only one other person, are the same now as then; if I am hit on the right cheek, the reasons for turning the left remain the same. But our life has changed greatly through the growth of science and technological advance; problems have thus been created for us which Scripture in no way anticipated. It may seem that there is a simple answer: everything can be taken back to the second great commandment, "You shall love your neighbor as yourself." But to tackle every situation which arises in our lives beginning from this would be both laborious and monotonous. We do not do this in the case of personal ethics. The New Testament provides examples of how in situations of that type the problems were resolved, and these may still help us in the solution of many of our problems of personal ethics, but we do not possess in the New Testament examples of equivalent situations for the complex relationships of modern life. Yet sometimes we can get back, as in the case of the slave-master relationship, to the underlying principles, and then advance from them to our own situation. There is no easy solution. It is probably true that when we try to understand these problems, or to preach about them, Scripture is not as much help as we would like it to be.

This brings us on to a related difficulty. If preaching is derived directly from Scripture, and if in the old sense of the word it is expository preaching, there is a danger that much of life may be left untouched; we may move only from the situations of Scripture to those which seem to be comparable situations in our daily lives with the result that vast areas of modern life remain untouched. Exactly the same is true when Scripture is used for devotional purposes; we read it and think of the problems which it raises as they relate to our own lives; since these problems relate almost entirely to personal ethics we may end up by living good lives within the area of personal ethics, but without much understanding of many of the major problems of our world. This is why so many devout Christians who have been reared on Scripture have little to say about social, industrial, political, and international problems, and when they do say something they talk as if these can be solved in a simple way as extensions of the problems of personal ethics, but they cannot be, for they are basically different.

In addition, as we have already hinted, there is one formal difference between our situation and that of Scripture which nothing we can do can overcome; Scripture is itself a part of our situation; indeed we might say that the whole history of the church is part of our situation. Earlier it was suggested that the very fact that a freezing of the tradition took place in Scripture modified the tradition itself. Here we have a similar idea. The only corresponding idea in Scripture is the relationship of the Old and New Testaments. The book of Amos is part of the situation for the New Testament writer that it never was

for Amos himself. Because the New Testament itself bears in our eyes
a certain authority it may lead us to do things that we would never
have thought of doing if we had to make a fresh approach to the
situation. If, as we have already suggested, there had been no reference in the New Testament to glossolalia it would probably never have
appeared in our culture for it is alien to it.[14] If Christological doctrine
had not already been framed in the terms of Chalcedon we would
never have thought of expressing it in those terms for those terms are
not the terms of our culture. We are the heirs of the past; it is part
of our situation; consequently our situation can never be the same as
that of the first Christians, or indeed of any Christians prior to our
time.

Finally it is important to realize that not merely do we have
different situations in many instances from those of Scripture, but we
live in a different culture. We have not only to make the transference
from one situation to another, but we have also to move from one
culture to another. And this is a deeper move. We have already seen
some of its consequences. They emerge even in personal ethics. Take
the case of abortion. The situation has changed not merely because
abortion can now take place safely and easily, but even more importantly because there is a change in culture with the rise of the belief
that what science can do safely and easily ought always to be done.
Our culture makes us see its problems in scientific terms and leads us
to solve them in exclusively scientific terms. This adds to many situations a dimension which is not found in Scripture.

(5) The next method of interpretation to which we turn is completely different from those at which we have already looked. Its basis
is purely theological; all theological statements in Scripture are to be
turned into anthropological statements. Since modern Western culture has no place for God Christians should live without God. This
has been understood in various ways. Some have simply said that
there is no God, and that therefore we can say nothing about him.
Others have said that we are not to think of God as simply present
in an old-fashioned kind of way to help man in his difficulties, either
by leading him out of trouble or as a stop-gap to fill in the points where
his rational thought cannot complete a solution to his understanding

of the world; what man still knows, and what is of supreme importance to him, is his own existence; therefore statements in Scripture
about the nature of God must be translated into statements about the
existence of man. If communication is to take place at all then there
must be some area in common between writer and reader, speaker and
hearer, in this case between the writers of Scripture and their present
day readers. If the activity of God and the concept of transcendence
are no longer shared between them, it is necessary to look elsewhere
for a common area. If God has disappeared out of ordinary life then
men can only find that common area in themselves, in the understanding of human existence that they all share. Because statements about
God cannot be expressed adequately in rational terms, but require the
use of "myth," and because science and philosophy have no place for
myth, it is impossible to talk properly about God. Statements about
God in Scripture are "mythological"; they must be translated into
existential and anthropological terms. We can make no statement
about God's absolute being, but only about his being for us, and such
a statement must be expressed in human terms. The statements of
Scripture if they are to be used in preaching or meditation must be
demythologized. It is important to grasp that this is a method of
moving from the text to today. Because the text is held within a
culture which accepts a God who is "active" in the world and because
our culture has no place for such a God we understand the text in a
way which excludes its God-reference. We translate it from theological into anthropological terms.

"Myth" is a term with a number of different meanings, or, better
perhaps, different stresses in its use. A story, like that of Santa Claus,
can be called a myth and the word then carries a strong nuance of
untruth: Santa Claus is not real but a "myth." More generally it can
be used of the expression of truth through a story: the fall of Adam
in Genesis 3 is a representation in story form of the sin of every man.
It can also be used as a means of explaining a truth which cannot
easily be expressed conceptually; when people say that God is "up
there" they are really saying something about his transcendence.
Finally the word "myth" often carried with it the sense of "primitive,
prescientific, non-rational." Only "primitive" (i.e. prescientific) man
would believe that in an eclipse of the sun it is swallowed by a dragon.

Whenever the term "demythologizing" is used many of these senses come into operation at different levels.

If demythologizing means the rejection of what is untrue then it must be accepted as a legitimate method of understanding Scripture. If it means the rejection of what is expressed prescientifically because it is expressed in such terms the conclusion is not so certain. The prescientific explanation may be, but not necessarily is, saying something which is true but not expressed in the way modern man would express it. Interesting here is the creation story of Genesis 1. On the one hand it has lost much of its "mythical" nature (where "mythical" = prescientific) but on the other it is not wholly freed from such language when compared with the earlier creation stories from which it was derived. In Genesis 1 it functions both as a "narrative" to explain the existence of the world and as a "hymn" celebrating God and creation. It can no longer be accepted as "explanation," and any attempt to accept it as such is disastrous, but does this mean it must be rejected as "hymn"? Much of our secular poetry is written in non-scientific terms and we do not reject it. If we accept Genesis 1 in that way we would be implying that the relation of God to the world as creator is not something which can be expressed in logically defensible statements understandable in scientific or historical terms but must be told in some other form, e.g., poetry or narrative (for the latter cf. Gen. 3). Recognizing the mythological element we might say that it is poetry and not science and can be retained as poetry but not as factual truth, or we might argue that since God is by definition outside scientific examination, truth about him can only be expressed "mythologically," but the type of mythology may need to be changed so that, for example, we no longer speak of God "up there" since no one believes that heaven is above us, but instead of God "out there" or of God "within," or we might say that we can only use statements which have scientific meaning, and so exclude all statements about God and talk only about ourselves.

To distinguish and choose between these three approaches (and there are probably other alternatives) would take us far outside the scope of our present purpose since to do so would require us to solve deep theological problems; all we wish to do here is examine the view that "translation" of the language of Scripture into the language of our world means its expression in scientific or anthropological terms. Our main reason for drawing attention to this method of interpretation is to point out how a theological position can control the way Scripture is understood. It is interesting that when those who rigorously adopt a theological demythologizing position turn to preaching, the result is often very similar to what happens when those who do not adopt this position also preach. But there is one reservation to be made. Those who attempt to preach in a purely demythological manner, or to express themselves only in existentialist terms, are restricted in the themes which they can use; they can only talk about man and his piety and not about God and his goodness; thus, while at points they sound the same as those who do not adopt their position, yet their preaching covers a much narrower area, and it often seems to end up with the same few themes, e.g., the need for decision, deliverance from anxiety.

All interpretation of Scripture is controlled by the theology of the person who interprets. It may not be true that a particular interpreter has a consistent theological position; his theology may change; but his theology and world-view always control his interpretation. We have already discussed the threefold relation between the world-view of the writer of a particular piece of Scripture, the culture of today, and our world-view; our world-view and our interpretation of a passage interplay with one another. This now needs to be developed a little further. There are a number of world-views in Scripture but they possess a basic similarity, or at least those in the New Testament do. Does our world-view have to be the same as that of the world-views of the writers of Scripture? Those who demythologize often claim that they are in fact interpreting Paul and John in the way in which Paul and John would interpret themselves—existentially. In other parts of the New Testament the existentialist interpretation is much less prominent. Thus Paul and John are erected into a criterion, a canon within a canon, by which the remainder of Scripture is judged. Again we do not wish to argue for or against such a theological position but to point out that in a different way it is one into which without realizing it anyone may fall. Those who listen to a particular preacher over a lengthy period often discover that he has certain favorite books in the Bible to which he constantly returns and that there are also parts from which he rarely preaches. If we are interpreting Scripture for ourselves, we will often find that we keep returning to the same passages for help and guidance and that we leave untouched vast areas of Scripture. We have thus created for ourselves a canon within a canon. We find that we respond to certain writers within Scripture more easily than we respond to others. This may be a perfectly correct position; certain portions of Scripture are more valuable than others; but it is important that we should be consciously aware that we are making such a restriction within Scripture.

The second point to be made in regard to this existentialist interpretation is that it may look as if those who demythologize are in effect arguing that Christianity is to be held within our present culture. If culture is unwilling to make statements about God, and indeed has no place for him, then our expression of Christianity should make no statements about him and should restrict itself to statements about ourselves. Those who demythologize would firmly deny that they accommodate themselves to modern culture. They would point to many differences between what they say about man and what culture implies about man, e.g., culture requires that a man's worth be evaluated in terms of his power or financial prosperity, whereas a Christian existential or anthropological interpretation can see a man's importance in his weakness. There is an ever changing and very deep problem here. On the one hand we cannot accept *in toto* the world-view of any particular writer of Scripture; on the other hand, we cannot permit Scripture to be interpreted wholly within any culture. The interpreter will reject certain aspects of culture; yet if he rejects the whole he may find himself with no point of contact between his interpretation and the world in which he lives. There is also a counter danger. If we expound by demythologizing and translate all statements into terms of general human existence we may free the biblical text from its ancient culture but we may not embed it in today's culture. It may be left in too abstract a form to speak to the actual condition of man.

A third aspect of this problem arises in a special way for the preacher, but also in part for those who interpret Scripture for themselves, in particular when they do so in a study group or Bible class. The person who has been trained as a minister has developed a world-

view which to a great extent he holds consciously and which he has
developed by thinking about various theological issues. But those to
whom he interprets have not had this advantage, or disadvantage. A
concrete example will show what is meant. During his theological
education the preacher will have come to understand the problem of
miracles and will have decided that either he can find a place for all
of them in his theology, or for some of them, or for none of them. But
in his congregation there will be those to whom a miracle creates no
problem because they have never realized there are problems, and at
the other extreme there will be those who reject all miracles because
they do not seem to have any place in modern thought. If the preacher
takes a miracle and "spiritualizes" it he may be accused by some of
not believing in its true nature, and by others of accepting it, because
since he does not deny its truth it appears to them that he has accepted
it. How is the preacher to interpret a passage in the terms of his own
world-view when he knows that the world-views of those who listen
to him may be different, and different in many varying ways among
themselves, from his own? He can probably get nowhere unless he
consciously realizes that the problem exists. He may then be able to
make some allowance for it and, where the differences are not acute
in matters essential to the faith, he may be able to make allowances
for those who differ from him.

(6) We deal now with what is more clearly a technique for adapting a text to fit a modern situation. It can be termed *substitution*. A
few examples will show what is meant and illustrate that everyone
carries out this process when applying the Scriptures to himself. In
Galatians 5:19–21 Paul gives a list of the works of the flesh; some of
these are universal, i.e., they are temptations for everyone: jealousy,
anger, envy. Some of them, however, are very limited and apply much
more to the culture of Paul's own time, e.g., idolatry, sorcery; while
the latter may still exist in our midst they are not widespread. It seems
perfectly legitimate to substitute for them temptations which are prev-
alent in our culture. Similarly in a passage like 1 Timothy 2:1–2 "I
urge that supplications, prayers, intercessions, and thanksgivings be
made for all men, for kings and all who are in high position . . . ,"
we may substitute any of "queen, president, prime minister" for
"king."

The next illustration is somewhat longer, and concerns the parable of Luke 14:16–24:

> But he said to him. "A man once gave a great banquet, and invited many; and at the time for the banquet he sent his servant to say to those who had been invited, 'Come; for all is now ready.' But they all alike began to make excuses. The first said to him, 'I have bought a field, and I must go out and see it; I pray you, have me excused.' And another said, 'I have bought five yoke of oxen, and I go to examine them; I pray you, have me excused.' And another said, 'I have married a wife, and therefore I cannot come.' So the servant came and reported this to his master. Then the householder in anger said to his servant, 'Go out quickly to the streets and lanes of the city, and bring in the poor and maimed and blind and lame.' And the servant said, 'Sir, what you commanded has been done, and still there is room.' And the master said to the servant, 'Go out to the highways and hedges, and compel people to come in, that my house may be filled. For I tell you, none of those men who were invited shall taste my banquet.' "

This parable reappears in the Gospel of Thomas § 64 and we find some substitutions made:

> Jesus said: A man had guests, and when he had prepared the dinner he sent his servant to summon the guests. He came to the first; he said to him: My master summons thee. He said: I have money with some merchants. They are coming to me in the evening. I will go and give them orders. I pray to be excused from the dinner. He went to another; he said to him: My master has summoned thee. He said to him: I have bought a house, and they ask me for a day. I shall not have time. He came to another; he said to him: My master summons thee. He said to him: My friend is about to be married, and I am to hold a dinner. I shall not be able to come. I pray to be excused from the dinner. He went to another; he said to him: My master summons thee. He said to him: I have bought a village; I go to collect the rent. I shall not be able to come. I pray to be excused. The servant came, he said to his master: Those whom thou didst summon to the dinner have excused themselves. The master said to his servant: Go out to the roads. Bring those whom thou shalt find, that they may dine. The buyers and the merchants [shall] not [enter] the places of my Father.[15]

What has happened here is that in the course of the transmission of the tradition various preachers in using it have modified it to suit the situations of their own congregations; here it has been given an urban setting instead of a rural. This is something that every preacher does and no one faults him for it.

Thus substitution is a perfectly satisfactory method of adapting Scripture to the modern situation, so long as the adaptation lies in line with the intention of the original author. In the examples given this is naturally so. But now we need to look at some others.

(a) There are in the Gospels a number of exorcism stories where Jesus casts out demons. While there are still many people who believe in the existence of demons and believe that exorcism should continue to be practiced, most people do not reckon seriously with the existence of demons in ordinary life and when they come to understand these passages they tend to talk about something other than actual demons. In earlier days preachers regularly referred to "the demon of drink"; and it is not so long since many preachers were describing the German nation as possessed by a Nazi demon. Those may be colorful illustrations but they are inadequate substitutions. We can see this at once when we ask how we deal with the alcoholic and the Nazi-possessed nation. The alcoholic is slowly "dried out," not exorcised. The nation possessed by the Nazi spirit is attacked with physical force, not prayer; a spiritual force cannot be outgunned. These then are not legitimate substitutions. Nor is it sufficient to think in terms of "evil influences"; these undoubtedly exist but they are not "supernatural"; they normally emanate from people either as individuals or as groups.

(b) In his letters Paul regularly refers to spiritual powers, principalities, authorities. In the ancient world these were believed to govern life in a much similar way to that in which today a believer in astrology imagines that his life is controlled by the stars. Paul argues that Christ has won a victory over these powers in his cross and that at the last they will all be subjected to him. We have no exact parallel in our situation and this has led to attempts to make substitutions. One often used is that of "blind economic forces," another "the spirit of unrest" which seems to pervade nations so that for no apparent reason strikes and civil disruption break out. But the attitude taken to economic forces or the spirit of unrest is quite different from that which Paul took to the spiritual powers of his time. We do not really believe that the economic forces are ungovernable nor that the spirit of unrest cannot be pacified and we seek political and economic solutions; we argue and reason and, apart from individual moments of despair, do not really believe that these forces and spirits are ultimately beyond our control. The readers of Ephesians were exhorted to fight against them with spiritual weapons, e.g., prayer. When Christians today pray for solutions to problems which face them, they pray that governments may take the right action; one does not simply pray, believing that by prayer alone the forces will disappear. Christians believe that something must be done about these forces now; they do not simply leave them to meet their end in subjection to Christ at his return. Moreover while it is relatively easy to see how Christ can be said to overcome a personal power of evil it is much more difficult to understand how a blind impersonal economic force can be made subject to him; in a new world we would expect it to disappear altogether.

(c) This reference to the return of Christ suggests the next example. Almost all Christians in the first couple of generations believed that the world was near its end. There are many references in the New Testament to this eschatological pressure; what is to be made of them? Few today take them literally; whatever they may say in public they do not in private imagine that there is any possibility of the world ending in this decade. We take an illustration from an actual sermon by Cardinal Newman in which he uses as his text Romans 13:11, "Now it is high time to awake out of sleep."[16] In the course of this sermon, which in the edition used is entitled "Self Denial: The Test of Religious Earnestness," he pleads for a more devout practice of self-denial on the part of Christians. But he ignores the context of his text; for the verse proceeds, "for salvation is nearer to us now than when we first believed; the night is far gone, the day is at hand." Paul based his exhortation upon his belief that the period until the return of Christ was short. Newman simply ignores this. In other words, he de-eschatologizes the text. A much more common way of dealing with a text like this, however, is to alter the eschatology from its cosmic orientation to a personal one. Instead of thinking of the judgment which may come with Christ's advent, emphasis is laid on the judgment which falls on every man at death. This still preserves the pressure. It seems a legitimate method of substitution in many instances, provided we accept the same concept of judgment after death as the early Christians had, though it eliminates the "social" aspect of biblical eschatology. However it is not a substitution which can be made universally. In writing about marriage in 1 Corinthians Paul says that it is better for a person not to marry in view of the "impending distress," i.e., the end of the world, and because "the appointed time has grown very short." (7:26,29) If we substitute death for the end of the world in this reference it is made to teach universal celibacy! The whole of 1 Corinthians 7:29–31 is often used without due attention being given to its underlying eschatological basis; the Christian's attitude to the world is to be governed by his belief in its speedy passing away. If we change this and speak of the transitoriness of life we take a different meaning from Paul; an individual life may end but the institutions of society are relatively stable; the individual may die but neither government as such nor the family as such are passing away.

(d) The final example is that of idolatry. There are many references in Scripture to the worship of idols and preachers have regularly substituted modern equivalents for ancient idols. They have argued that instead of bowing down to wood and stone, men now bow down to wealth, success, ambition, power; there is no end of the substitutions which are made. This kind of substitution may possibly be defended if we are prepared to define God as the area of our deepest concern, for wealth or success can easily become a man's deepest concern. It is by no means certain that this is an adequate definition of God for it defines him in human terms in relation to ourselves and seems to omit any conception of transcendence. We need to examine the substitution more carefully. The preacher who speaks of wealth or success as an idol tends to think of these as taking possession of the entire life of the man who worships them. This was rarely the attitude of the pagan to his idols. While there were some devotees, as in the worship of Dionysus, who gave themselves up entirely to their god, for the majority of pagans their worship was only a part of their lives. They worshiped their idol so that through him they might be able to prosper in this world, or at least be preserved from disaster, and live on in the world to come. But the man who worships wealth or success never believes that this will help him in the next world, though it may enable him to prosper in this. The pagan who worshiped his god worshiped him in order that he might receive something from him; if, however, a man worships success or wealth for some other purpose, then by the very nature of the argument it would be this other purpose which is his idol and not success or wealth. The idolatrous worshiper never restricted himself to one god; he had a multiplicity of gods; the man who is alleged to make wealth or success his idol has by definition a single object. Again the idolatrous worshiper only devoted a portion of his life to his god or gods; his religion made no claim to embrace the whole of his life, and the argument is that wealth or ambition dominates the whole life. Finally, because the idolator recognized the transcendent element in life it was possible to appeal to him to turn from his idols to the living and true God; the man gripped by wealth or success does not necessarily have any sense of a transcendent factor. Three more points may be made: (i) While idolatry may disappear, and has disappeared in many parts of the world, it is difficult to conceive of continued civilized existence without money or something similar to it and without some men being placed in positions of importance, even if they are utterly without ambition. (ii) Preachers normally direct their attacks on idolatry at the members of their congregations rather than at unbelievers; the implication is that believers may have idols alongside God and divide their worship; but in the world of the Bible it was God *or* idols; the Christian was one who had turned from idols (1 Thess. 1:9f). Had idols a real place in our culture we would not be forced to try and think up substitutions for them in texts.[17] (iii) If our real desire is to attack the dangers of wealth and ambition there are plenty of straightforward texts which will fulfil the purpose: "You cannot serve God and mammon" (Matt. 6:24; cf. Luke 6:24); there is no need to play tricks with others in order to launch the attack.

If we now look back and ask why some of these substitutions are exegetically defective we see that three of them, demons, spiritual powers, idols, derive from the culture of the ancient world and are not a part of the culture of our world. The fourth, eschatological pressure, derives from a factor belonging to the world-view of the first Christians, their expectancy of a speedy return of Christ, and it does not belong to the world-view of most Christians today. The problem in exegesis is thus created for us by changes in culture and world-view. Because Christianity arose within a certain culture, Scripture was formed in terms appropriate to an understanding in that culture. We cannot move easily from the assumptions of that culture to the assumptions of our own culture. A more careful exegesis than simple substitution is required. Substitution is a snare to those who believe that every part of Scripture is relevant to us today. If 666, the number of the beast, originally meant Nero, and this is by no means certain, then there must be some political or religious figure to whom it applies today. If Cyrus (Isa. 45:1ff) can be seen as God's servant in punishing Israel, is Chairman Mao (or some equivalent figure) to be viewed in the same way as God's punishment for Christianity or the white race?

(7) Another technique in which we move from the text to its understanding is *universalization*. The selected text or passage which was set originally in one situation is now interpreted so as to apply to a whole range of situations and circumstances. There are, of course, many universal statements in the New Testament, though they are fewer than is sometimes imagined. Many of those that appear to lack a concrete context do so only because they have already been universalized; the early church quickly lost the concrete situation in which words of Jesus were spoken and passed them on in its oral tradition without such a concrete situation; sometimes it supplied a fresh concrete situation.[18] The saying in Mark 8:35, " 'for whoever would save his life will lose it; and whoever loses his life for my sake and the gospel's will save it,' " is a more or less universal statement; it speaks of discipleship to Jesus. Probably its original form, as we can learn from parallels in the other Gospels, was "for whoever would save his life will lose it; and whoever loses his life will save it." It had a concrete situation when Jesus spoke it and may have referred to literal martyrdom. The new concrete situation in Mark is that of membership in the church; within that area it seems to be a universal statement. The saying of Jesus immediately preceding it in Mark (8:34), " 'If any man would come after me, let him deny himself and take up his cross and follow me,' " while apparently universal was actually once concrete. The reference to the cross is picked up by all Christians today and is rarely given a physical connotation but taken metaphorically; in its original context the saying will probably have referred to a literal cross, a not infrequent object in the world of the disciples; in order to universalize it we have to regard it as a metaphor, and within

the Christian context where we understand it as a reference to the cross of Jesus it is easy to do this.

The process of universalization can be illustrated from a sermon of F. W. Robertson.[19] In this he takes the story of Luke 12:13–14 in which a man asks Jesus to compel his brother to divide his inheritance with him and Jesus refuses. Robertson begins with an introductory section in which he says that if Jesus came among us today we would reject him in the same way as the Pharisees and the Sadduccees did in his own day. Here we have a straight transference of the situation of the first century to the nineteenth, yet this straight transference is not as simple as it looks. Studdart Kennedy in his famous poem about the coming of Jesus to Birmingham suggested that we would not deliberately reject Jesus but simply ignore him, leaving him to stand alone in the rain. But Robertson's main point is that since Jesus refused to interfere in the case of the two brothers the church should be very wary of interfering in politics. Christianity may determine general issues, but it should not become involved in particular political incidents. He applies this directly to a question of his own day: the relation of peasants and landlords in respect of the ownership of land. Christ's kingdom was spiritual and not legal and the church should not take sides in a matter of this nature. Jesus refused to be a friend to one of the two brothers so that he might be a friend to both; the church, therefore, must not support one class in the class struggle, so that it may be free to be the friend of both classes. Finally, Robertson makes another universalization. Because in Luke 12:15 Jesus goes on to say that men should beware of covetousness he concludes that what divides nations and classes is covetousness. There are clearly other factors involved in the divisions within and between nations.

Robertson has moved from a simple situation involving only two people to the complex social, political, and national issues which continually perplex politicians and citizens and he has assumed that he can use a simple situation to deal with the more complex political situation. In 1 Corinthians 6:1–8 Paul deals with some of the Corinthian converts who have gone to law with one another, and he tells the church that it ought to be the judge in these matters. If we worked in the same way as Robertson, we could quite easily universalize this advice of Paul and say that the church ought to act as judge in all

social, political, and national problems. We would then have a blatant
contradiction with Robertson's universalization. This contradiction
arises directly because of the two universalizations; in neither case is
sufficient attention paid to the contextual nature of the advice given
by Jesus and Paul. In the case of Paul we do not know the kind of
issues which individual Christians had against one another and which
led them to go to law. In the case of Jesus we cannot know the
situation which drove one brother to approach Jesus, nor anything of
the circumstances in which the inheritance was left to the other
brother. If one concrete situation can be universalized into a desired
conclusion, it is almost always possible to take another concrete situation and universalize it into a directly opposite conclusion. It is the
process of universalization which is dangerous. It forgets that Scripture invariably belongs in concrete situations.

Another way in which universalization takes place is through the
derivation of general laws, moral principles, or dogmatic propositions
from statements and incidents in Scripture.

Harry Emerson Fosdick has a sermon on Matthew 6:32f, "Your
heavenly Father knoweth that ye have need of all these things. But
seek ye first his kingdom, and his righteousness; all these things shall
be added on to you."[20] The sermon is given the title "Righteousness
First!" and this is where the emphasis lies. It is, he argues, important
both for individuals, and he instances newlyweds, and for nations (the
sermon was written during World War II) to accept the basic law,
"seek righteousness first." It is important to note that in universalizing this into a "basic law" (Fosdick's term) he has simplified the text.
Jesus said that men were to seek God's kingdom and God's righteousness. Fosdick has omitted all reference to God's kingdom. He has thus
removed from the text its eschatological feature and it is only because
he has done this that he can make it into a law. Seeking God's
kingdom cannot be made into a law. But he has also laid the emphasis,
not on God's righteousness as Jesus did, but on human righteousness.
Righteousness becomes an abstract principle which men are to seek,
rather than God's righteousness. Once a text has been reduced to a
basic moral principle like this, it is possible to apply it to anything.
It is at least arguable that love is a more important basic moral
principle for newlyweds and mercy for nations in a state of war than
righteousness.

Newman in a sermon on John 13:17, "If you know these things, blessed are you if you do them," lays the emphasis on knowledge and obedience.[21] Religion consists in these. Throughout the sermon he never once asks what in the context of John 13 "these things" means. In effect he withdraws the verse from its context and then universalizes it into a religious principle and in the end makes it mean that earnestness and sincerity are all that is necessary to religion. The text has become a principle which can be applied generally.

If we read the commentaries of the Puritan Divines we find that they often do this. They take one by one the sentences of a passage in Scripture and erect each into a dogmatic statement from which they then make deductions. Scripture is here treated as a compilation of universalized dogmatic statements, and its contextual nature is lost.

If Scripture belongs to a culture or cultures, then it is even more difficult to universalize. A universal statement in one culture may not be a universal statement in another. In universalizing Matthew 6:33 Fosdick forgot that Jesus' statement was part of a Christian and Jewish sub-culture, or of a common Jewish and Christian world-view. He ignored the eschatological sub-culture and so produced a moral principle for our culture.

There is one further criticism of "universalizing" which has to be made, and it applies also to allegorization and in large part to "substitutionism": these methods deal with the words of Scripture. They seek by some verbal trick to apply the words of Scripture to a new situation. We have argued that Scripture is a "freezing" of the tradition about Jesus, a crystallization of the "Word"; it is Jesus, or the Word, who has to come into our situation, and verbal tricks will not free him or it. Useful at times as they may be they have to be used extremely carefully. It is perhaps the easiness of their use and the apparent cleverness of the trick which makes them attractive. For this reason we should beware of them. God cannot be brought to men by verbal dexterity.

(8) Closely related to universalization is *identification*. This is the process in which we identify ourselves, or our group, with a character or group of people in Scripture. As an example to show what is intended we select the story of the paralyzed man who was carried by four friends to Jesus (Mark 2:1–12); he was in a house and they were

unable to enter because it was crammed full of people; so the four
broke open the roof and let the man down; Jesus forgave the man his
sins and healed him; the scribes complained that he was acting blas-
phemously. We meet different people in this story: the paralyzed man,
the four faithful friends, the householder whose roof was destroyed,
the Scribes who complained. The question is then asked: "With whom
do you identify?"[22] In this kind of approach there is the hidden
assumption that each one of us must identify with some person or
group in the story. This is a false assumption. In any case we can be
sure that in this story Jesus did not heal the man so that we should
mirror ourselves in the attitude of one of those standing around nor
did Mark record it for that purpose; there is no justification for using
it in that way at all.

Having said so much quite clearly there are cases where identification is the true and proper method of opening up a text or passage.
Identification with Adam is an instance. The word "Adam" is the
same as one of the Hebrew words for man; the story of Adam and his
fall was intended by the writer of Genesis to tell us something about
the sin of every man; if we then follow the intention of the author we
identify ourselves with Adam and see in him our weakness when
placed before temptation. Equally those passages in Scripture which
speak of man as sinner and in need of God's grace can be used in this
way; we identify ourselves with the sinner. But now it is necessary to
be more careful; if the passage comes in a story then the sin of the man
described is identified as particular sins; there is no reason to suppose
that these are our sins. Our identification can only be with man as
sinner, not with a particular man's sins. Too explicit an identification
can lead to some people contracting out. There can be a perverse
movement from "These are not my sins" to "I am not a sinner."

It is important here to break in and direct attention briefly to the
use of biblical characters in our understanding of ourselves. It is very
difficult to be certain of the true characters of those who appear in
Scripture since we have so little material about them; too much has
to be left to the imagination. Most of the material we do possess has
been recorded for a purpose other than that of giving us information
about the particular person; the Bible does not share our interest in
the development of personality. Peter will serve as an example; what

we find in the New Testament about him has often been used to argue that under pressure he was a weak character. This is not so obvious as it seems. The incidents in which the weakness of Peter are shown are not recorded primarily to tell us about Peter's weakness but about the mercy of God who forgives him and the strength of God which, when he repents, can sustain him. There would have been no point in the evangelist recounting incidents in which Peter was strong if his purpose was to show the mercy and strength of God. Thus the selection of incidents which we have been given about Peter has been dominated by an interest other than the character of Peter himself. It is foolish of us therefore to use these incidents to build up a picture of the character of Peter and then to go on and apply it to men generally. We ought to use the incidents of Peter's weakness instead to argue for God's mercy and strength. But even if we could depict adequately the character of someone who features in a Bible story it would still be wrong to universalize him. "Dare to be a Daniel" is erroneous advice in many delicate personal situations. Those who are already like Mary tend to feed on her character while those who are already like Martha feed on hers; we can choose the character we like and use it to intensify characteristics which we already possess when in fact we need other characteristics.

To return to the more general technique of identification, an incident frequently used in this way is the crucifixion. There were many groups involved in the trial and execution of Jesus and none of them come out of it very well. One disciple betrayed Jesus, another denied him, and the rest ran away. Judas was moved by greed (or was it? we really know so little about Judas' motives, and our ignorance here is an illustration of the dangers of the identification method). The priests wanted to get rid of a possible threat to their position, and the Pharisees saw their reputation as holy and devout men under criticism through Jesus' life. The crowds welcomed him when he first came to Jerusalem but were easily maneuvered into crying for his crucifixion. Pilate recognized that Jesus was a good man but he also had to be careful not to endanger his employment. Only the centurion comes out reasonably well. "Were you there when they crucified my Lord?" Yes, certainly; but my sins may not lie in any of the categories of those who were present at the actual crucifixion. When I am unwilling to pay enough for my sugar to those who cultivate it in the West Indies, or when my representatives manipulate the internal politics of another state to keep a capitalist oppressive regime in power, it is Jesus whom I crucify. Yes, I was there when my Lord was crucified, but not as Peter or Pilate or Caiaphas. It would be men with different sins who would crucify Jesus today. Identification may never bring home my position to me as concrete sinner if it is drawn too rigidly. By forcing me into a precast mold it may miss reaching my soul. In the final analysis identification runs the danger of neglecting the situational and cultural embedding of each biblical story and it cannot escape this danger since it necessarily operates from individual concrete accounts of people and events.

The basic error in the way this technique is sometimes used can be seen once we realize that it can be carried through just as effectively by starting from nonbiblical stories. Snow White and the Seven Dwarfs in the Disney version provides an excellent base for its exercise. There is the little community of the seven, each with his own peculiarities which can breed trouble among them. Snow White is their savior, the wicked step-mother Satan. We can identify as easily with one of the dwarfs as with one of the characters in a biblical story; anyone who doubts this should recollect how after the film was first extensively shown those who had seen it went round identifying themselves and their friends with the different dwarfs. The stories of the Bible were not told to illustrate character but to awaken their hearers to the judgment and love of God. Concentration on "identification" and the consequent production of moral lessons can lead us to missing what Scripture is really about. The story of Ruth was not told originally to inspire in women a desire to be like Ruth but to deal with a situation in which an exclusiveness was in danger of controlling Judaism; even David had a non-Jew in his immediate ancestry! In any case those who idealize Ruth rarely remember to tell their audiences how she got into Boaz's bed by stealth and committed him to a marriage he might not otherwise have been willing to make.

(9) A method which moves in an entirely different area is that of *imaginative re-creation*. This exists in at least two forms. The first is quite straightforward. The imagination is used to build up the back-

ground—to re-create the Palestinian scene for the sayings and actions of Jesus or the Corinthian scene for the stories of the church there. This is very valuable but it also has its difficulties and dangers. The value does not just lie in the portrayal of what life was like in those days but also in the way it lets us see how remote the world of the Bible is from us; thereby it brings home to us that we cannot simply take up biblical passages and apply them to ourselves. Consequently it has for the ordinary church member or reader of the Bible the value which the historical-critical method has for the theological student— it shows him the gap between his world and that of the Bible. Through archaeological and historical research we now know much more about the ancient world than was known a century ago and there are plenty of good books which supply this information. Some of the books which do it, though, cut corners and do not always show the differences; they stress the similarities. This brings us to the dangers. The greatest danger is that we take an interest in the background as background; a knowledge of the sex-life of Corinth is enthralling (and quite a lot is known about it) but it may only titillate us instead of bringing us the Word of God. Another almost equally serious danger is that through only knowing a little we may misplace the background. A sermon by A.J. Gossip provides an example. It begins by talking about the way Mary brought up Jesus and then goes on to his early life in Nazareth:

> What are you going to be, the boys would say to one another, as they trooped home from school, to Him among the rest. And He would answer, "Oh! I have to go into the workshop." And He did, while others went to college and became successful men; in course of time [they] would come home for a holiday to the old village they had quite out-grown: and folk would tell each other how well they had done, and what a credit they were to the little town. While Jesus all the time was just the carpenter, whom they ordered about, and of whom they expected sheer impossibilities, being no doubt just as fussy and as selfish and as unreasonably insistent that they must be attended to at once, whoever had to wait, as are the rest of us.[23]

That is a perfectly good picture of what the boys would be like in a small Scottish town at the end of last century or the beginning of this; they were encouraged to push themselves ahead through school so that they could get away and be successful. But there were no opportunities like that in Palestine in Jesus' day; everybody stayed at home; and probably many of his fellows envied Jesus because at least he had a trade and would always have secure employment. Gossip uses his imagination to try and build up a picture of Jesus' character and because he got the "archaeology" wrong there is no guarantee he got the character right.

This brings us on to the second, and much more important way, in which imagination is used to re-create, namely to re-create character: through the imagination we enter sympathetically into the life of another person. This is something we do every day when we try to understand the behavior of others. We believe we can do it because basically we and others are human beings with the same ways of thinking, feeling, and acting, and since human nature has not changed in that respect from the first century we can enter sympathetically into what happened to people then and know what made them tick. This brings us very close to what we have been just looking at—the use of material about people in Scripture. Since we know so little about them and since even the little information we do possess was given to us for reasons other than character analysis, we run the danger of letting our imaginations fly away into all kinds of airy fancies; the less one knows, the easier it is to be imaginative, witness the multitude of character studies of Judas. From the second century onwards Christians have used their imagination to fill in gaps in Jesus' life; they did this in particular in relation to his early years, as Gossip did in the illustration above. They were able to do this because nothing is known about his life during that period. In the early centuries they filled it largely with stories of miracles which he performed as a boy. Their age liked such stories and so they were supplied. Ours does not, and so those among us who write about these years tend to idealize his childhood and fill it with his innocent charm and open-eyed wonder at what was happening around him. The qualities which religious people would like to see in themselves they see in him.

There are two other serious points here. The first concerns Jesus and the second the imaginative entering into the character of anyone from a distant age and culture. We take the second first. While we have emotions and minds and wills just as men of old had, it is not quite true to say that we think and feel and will as they would have done. We have already referred to the corporate personality of the family and of mankind as a whole. We can look from outside and say that the ancients adopted a particular attitude because of their idea of corporate personality, but to enter into the life of a person for whom this is not a theory but part of the way he lives probably requires an act of empathy beyond anything we can achieve. We can appreciate Darius' desire to punish those who tried to entrap Daniel but we do not instinctively feel with him in his decree that their wives and children should be punished with them. The Eskimo cannot enter sympathetically into the attitude towards the animal world of the Palestinian, and our whole attitude to nature was profoundly modified by the Romantic Revival of the late eighteenth and early nineteenth centuries; we will naturally bring our new outlook to those parts of Scripture where it seems to us that nature is glorified. Again if a man of the twentieth century has no place in his life for the transcendent, while he can understand that a first century man had this and therefore see why he thought or acted in some particular way, yet he cannot enter into the experience of that person in a real way. He can observe his reverence before "fate" or "the stars" but he cannot share sympathetically in it. Cultural change, then, may make it more difficult for us to enter sympathetically into the first century than would appear at first sight. We are afraid, ambitious, lustful, kindly, as men of old were, but culture conditions us to be such in different ways. There is no stripped down "basic man" but always man who belongs to a particular culture. An illustration of this is the difficulty many heterosexuals have in understanding homosexuals; they realize they have a real experience but cannot appreciate what it actually is.

The second point relates to the use of the imagination to re-create, not character in general, but specifically that of Jesus. The basis of its use is again the fact of our common humanity. If we apply this to Jesus then we are making a theological judgment. It can be put simply in this way: if we say we know how Jesus thought we are clearly using our own experience as a guide because there is practically no record of his thoughts in Scripture; if we regard him as in some way different from other men, e.g., as one who can work miracles which we cannot do, then his nature is different from ours; we have no common basis on which our creative imagination may enter into his personality. The same is true if we regard him as sinless. The one thing which the rest of humanity shares is its sinfulness, and when we attempt to enter imaginatively into the lives of others one factor which crops up again and again is our common sinfulness. We try to understand people who go wrong and we can succeed at least partially because we ourselves go wrong from time to time. But can we understand a sinless personality? It is not necessary now to make a theological judgment about Jesus as a miracle-worker or as sinless, but only to say that if we apply imaginative re-creation to him then we are making a theological judgment implying that he is in every way human; it is important to ensure that this judgment is consistent with other theological judgments about him which we make from time to time.

4
conclusion

It is necessary now to draw together some of what has been said, stress again some elements in it, and draw some conclusions.

(1) We must know ourselves. We are the vital link between that which, or he who, precipitates himself in Scripture and the understanding which we convey to others. Each of us approaches Scripture with his own, or her own, presuppositions. These presuppositions are part of our world-view, part of our personal theology. In the first instance they relate to the way we regard Scripture. Does it consist of infallible propositions? Is it the record of certain acts of God? Is it an inspired record? Is there revelation outside Scripture? Our views here will dictate how we handle the text. Secondly, we have much wider presuppositions arising from our Christian faith. How does God act in our world? Did he once intervene to perform miracles? Does he still intervene? Does he intervene directly in nature or through men's minds? Is the world likely to end shortly? Will the world continue indefinitely? Has God an ultimate purpose for the world? Is there one soteriological theory of the death of Jesus which ought to govern and control our view of the cross or are there a number of theories? Is Jesus truly God and man? Can man in any way escape the snares of temptation without knowledge of Christ? Thirdly, we share in the culture of the world in which we live. What value do we give to education? Do we believe that technology can help us deal with some or all of the world's problems? Is it good for scientists to investigate without restriction the world in which we live? Are our disagree-

ments to be settled by discussion or by authority? Has political life
become too debased for a good man to take any part in it? Is it basic
to man's nature that he has a right to have employment?

These are only a few of the questions which may reveal the presuppositions operating in our minds when we come to understand Scripture. Our minds are not empty when we read or listen to Scripture;
what we hear is already partly predetermined by what is already in
them; our presuppositions shape what we understand. It is not necessary to argue here for any one particular set of presuppositions, but
to insist that we become aware of our own so that when we understand
and interpret we know how we are being influenced by them. It is also
important that we see that our presuppositions are consistent, that we
do not operate with one set at one time, and with another at another.
If we believe that the teaching of Jesus, rather than the interpretation
of the New Testament writers, is primary we ought not to use the
interpretation of the parable of the sower but the parable itself. If we
believe that an event (e.g., Jesus' stilling of the storm at sea) did not
take place, we should not draw spiritual lessons from it.

As well as presuppositions we all have particular interests and
these interests often determine how we understand Scripture. It is
remarkable when reading even some of the greatest of preachers to
discover how often their sermons, commencing with very diverse
texts, are directed again and again to making the same point. If we
are ecumenically minded our sermons may end too often in ecumenical lessons; if we are anti-ecumenical they may too often end as attacks
on the ecumenical movement. Congregations are not fed when the
same tune is always played. We need then to be conscious of our own
interests. If we fail to be aware of them they will operate to limit the
full width of the understanding of God and of man which can emerge
from Scripture. Again it is not necessary to argue that certain interests
ought to prevail in the mind of one who comes to understand Scripture, but rather to warn each who comes to beware lest his interests
blind him to the whole of what God says.

(2) If we want to understand Scripture so that we may communicate our understanding to others, then we have to remember that the
presuppositions and interests of others may differ from ours. If our

minds are not empty when we come to interpret, the minds of our hearers are not empty when they come to listen; their presuppositions and their interests determine what they hear in what we say. We have already seen how this can affect the way in which a preacher deals with the miracles. But it is much wider than this. Apart from what happens in sermons, within any group that meets for discussion there will be some who wish to take sections of the Bible more literally than others do. There are few people who in practice wish to place the same stress on every section of Scripture. Some may emphasize very heavily those passages which insist on individual repentance and conversion; others those which relate to poverty and its value for the Christian. Their differing emphases arise out of their differing presuppositions about evangelism and poverty. But unless we are aware that we have presuppositions and interests and other people have different presuppositions and interests, we shall only get annoyed with them for not seeing Scripture in the same way as we do and for closing their eyes to what seems to us its obvious meaning. This is related to the pluralism of our culture. What speaks to the condition of young people may mean nothing to older people; what is relevant to the sins and virtues of suburbia may utterly miss the mark in a run-down inner city area; yet all congregations contain both young and old and many those who come from different areas of the city.

The preacher shares a great deal of the situation of his hearers, though his theological training to some extent sets him apart. But he can begin with what he shares. The shared situation may be local, national, or even ecclesiastical. In the last case the Christian calendar ensures that preacher and people are thinking at the same time of the birth, death, or resurrection of Christ and sermons can center on this shared interest. Local situations are by their very nature so individual as to exclude general rules or procedure. A national situation might be an anniversary. In Scotland the birthday of the poet Robert Burns (January 25) coincides with the celebration of the conversion of the Apostle Paul. This provides an opportunity to look in a new way at the latter, for if anyone were to compare Paul in his pre-Christian days with Burns they would have seen in the former a devout servant of God and in the latter a profligate, yet it was the former who was converted and who afterwards saw God's hand in his conversion.

(3) Is it the first task of the preacher to find a suitable text? Must he always begin from a biblical passage? (We may leave aside questions of the extent of the passage, whether a single verse or a paragraph.) Ought books of the Bible to be gone through *seriatim?* Should a lectionary be used? The preacher at any rate ought to avoid merely using a text as a jumping-off ground for whatever he wants to say. If his sermon bears no real relation to his text, he is certainly better off without it. All we know of the preaching of New Testament times goes to suggest that its preachers did not use texts; this is true whether the sermons reported in Acts are authentic reproductions of actual sermons by Peter, Paul, and Stephen, or whether they represent the type of sermon which Luke, or whoever was the author of Acts, thought that Peter, Paul, and Stephen ought to have preached, or whether they represent the preaching practice of Luke's own day. Indeed it is worthy of note that Paul began his sermon in Athens not from a biblical text but from an inscription on a heathen altar, "To an unknown God." Now, of course, it might be said that the New Testament had not yet been written and therefore the early preachers can hardly be accused of not using it. But Scripture did exist for them in the Old Testament. They do not begin from it though they use it in their preaching. Through it they disclose God's ways of which Jesus was the fulfillment. No scriptural example or precept then binds us to the New Testament as our starting point; what binds us is that of which the New Testament is a series of crystallizations—Jesus Christ. But how can we start to preach without a text? A sermon could be directed in such a way that it ended with a text, which would then be brought in as a kind of climax. But that is not really what is intended here. The sermons in Acts bring in the Old Testament as they go along. This is almost certainly the approach we would have to make if we were treating some problem of the modern world; a sermon about euthanasia would refer to life as given by God and as held in responsibility towards him, but also in responsibility towards others so that they should neither be overburdened with care for those for whom there is no hope of recovery nor suddenly deprived of their help and guidance. There is rich biblical material to bring in at all these points; but the material would not just be used as proof texts (indeed to almost every "proof text" another can be produced to prove

the opposite!) but as illustrative of the ways of God with men and of men with one another.

Thus there are areas of life with which the preacher may wish to deal, and which he cannot easily reach with a text. He ought not to take a text and by making substitutions in it or by universalizing it, or by playing some other trick with it, make it relate to his predetermined subject. If he restricts himself to preaching through a book or using a lectionary, while he certainly gains by the widening of his perspective and is saved from hammering away at a limited field of ideas, he also runs the grave danger of forcing passages to relate to situations in our present existence when they may not properly be made to do so. There are questions which come to us out of our situations and culture which it is only possible to reach from the most general of texts like "love your neighbor as yourself." But it will be very monotonous if the preacher continually starts from the same general text. Yet in another sense he may often have to do this. Jesus Christ is the spring of Christian action. When Paul wants the Corinthians to contribute a bit more to the collection for the saints in Jerusalem he does not appeal to their sympathy with a vivid picture of poverty in Jerusalem but tells them that Jesus was born (2 Cor. 8:9; "he became poor" is a reference to the incarnation); he seeks a penny more from each member and he recalls them to the incarnation! When bitterness, rivalry, and self-interest marred the life of the Philippian church he does not advise them to pull together better but reminds them of him who being in the sphere of deity took human likeness and humbled himself and in obedience accepted death, even death on a cross (Phil. 2:1–11). When in a passage of tremendous power Paul has proclaimed the swallowing up of death in victory he ends with the almost banal advice to be steadfast, immovable, always abounding in the work of the Lord (1 Cor. 15:58). All Christian thought and life must continually be brought back to its center in Christ, but it is not always necessary to start from a text to do this.

If, however, a text is used then it must be correctly exegeted. When Jesus calls people to be his disciples he tells them to deny themselves (Mark 8:34). Often this is taken as if it said "deny this and that to themselves." Let the Christian deny himself certain pleasures so that he may more readily fulfil his mission—as Hitler denied himself tobacco and alcohol! But in the text "himself" is the direct object of "deny"; it is not pleasure or advancement or ambition which is to be denied, but the "self." This puts the meaning on another plane; in denying things to oneself the self may actually be affirmed as all important. Indeed the self can never really be denied by itself, so subtle are the temptations to affirm oneself. Therefore after seeing the true meaning of the words of the text they need to be set in their context—following Jesus; and this Jesus is one who gives his life as a ransom for men and defeats the devil and the power of evil. Within this context, that of the whole Gospel, the text can be not only understood but lived out.

Exact exegesis also means noticing where it is impossible to remain within the words or imagery of the text itself. When we talk about the righteousness of God and justification by faith we use terms drawn from the legal sphere and think of God as judge. To our minds this suggests a neutral and independent arbiter who settles issues by means of a fixed code of rules. The judge's impartiality is so important that in major cases he is expected to disqualify himself should he know one or other of the contending parties. But the Hebrew judge not only lived among those whose cases he tried but he was also expected to discover cases of injustice and set them right; he did not merely wait for them to be brought to him. His role was therefore much more active than that of a modern judge. This means that if God is a good judge, i.e., if he is righteous, he will be active to seek the good of men; if he is a righteous God he will be a Savior (Isa. 45:21; the righteousness and the salvation of God are often paralleled, cf. Isa. 61:10; Ps. 71:15). If we preach about the righteousness of God, without carefully explaining what is meant, we may convey the wrong idea, for our hearers will automatically think of a modern "neutral" judge. The biblical idea might be more adequately conveyed, remaining within the legal sphere, by speaking of a probation officer or social worker who seeks to win back from evil someone committed to his or her care. This image is itself deficient since it lacks the element of ultimate judicial decision but it may serve to open up a new understanding of God. Exact exegesis is not satisfied by the use of a strict verbal translation parallel but requires the imaginative use of truer contemporary parallels. As we try to think this through although we may go up many false trails we will continually be digging more deeply into the inexhaustible depths of God's activity in search of those who do wrong. Both the New English Bible's "here is revealed God's way of righting wrong" and the Good News Bible's "the gospel reveals how God puts people right with himself" (Rom. 1:17) bring out the essentially dynamic character of God which is lost in the King James rendering. Both however still require translation into an image or set of images which will speak to people today.

Exact exegesis however becomes difficult when we have to deal with texts which are in partial or total contradiction with one another. If the contradiction arises out of the differing situations of writers and original readers of the New Testament as is the case in relation to views of the state[1] then these situations can be clearly explained, but the contradiction may seem more basic. There is a series of passages which teach an eternal and unalterable division of mankind after death; there is also a smaller series which teaches a final reconciliation of all things to God (Col. 1:20; Eph. 1:10; Rom. 8:19–21; Phil. 2:9–11). It would be wrong merely to count the number of texts and give the decision to the majority. Each text is a crystallization of the tradition and we need to push behind the diverse crystallizations to the Christ whom they crystallize. That does not mean we go back to Jesus' actual words, always provided relevant sayings exist, for as we have them they are part of the crystallization, but back to him as the center of theology. What is the new element which with him has entered into thought? What difference has he made? When we put it this way we see that the larger group of texts continue traditional Jewish views and that the smaller group represents something new; further when we examine this smaller group we see that in three of them their view is directly linked to the position of Christ himself, i.e., it is a Christologically oriented position, and in the fourth (Rom. 8:19–21) there is an indirect linking. This suggests that in this group we possess the basic Christian view.[2]

What has been said in relation to the preacher holds equally true for the person who wishes to use Scripture for daily guidance and devotion. Certainly many of its passages can be transferred directly to his condition because they deal with the basic issues between man and God, but there are vast areas of daily experience which cannot easily be brought within the direct range of Scripture. It is necessary to remember there are those who have pioneered these areas and have begun to express in their writings what is the appropriate crystallization of the Christian tradition for them. We should be ready to use their writings lest we leave large areas of our lives not touched by God. To search out and use these writings is not to adopt a new method, though the writings themselves may be new. Past generations used the works of the great mystics for this purpose. Today many of these seem as remote, if not more remote, than Scripture itself. We need to use the works of living writers, whether mystics or prophets.

There is a related point. Even when we begin with a text or passage of Scripture and develop it for our own meditation, or for a sermon, we cannot separate it from the whole body of Scripture. Each text or passage must be seen in the light of all the revelation of God in Christ that we have in Scripture. Each text or passage reveals an aspect of our understanding of God and existence, but it is always only a limited aspect and needs to be held within the understanding we receive from other texts and passages. There is thus a continual interplay between the passage with which we are dealing and all the other passages we know. And, of course, there is the interplay with the Christian tradition to which we belong and with the world as we know it.

(4) This brings us to the crunch question: "How do we know whether an interpretation is right or wrong?" When we try to understand Scripture, when we frame our understanding in a sermon, then a new crystallization takes place of that which Scripture was itself a crystallization. We began in Chapter 1 by attempting to define Scripture rather than preaching. Our definition of preaching has now become apparent. It is the crystallization in our culture and our situation through our world-view of that which, or he who, was originally crystallized in the primitive hymns and creeds, the various books of Scripture and the history of the church. It is always bound by our situation and culture; that is why a sermon preached twenty years ago has to be rewritten to be used today and why those who preach occasionally in various pulpits to congregations they do not know rather than regularly to the same congregation find it difficult to speak in other than the most general terms. It is also why the

student who fears he has put the whole gospel into his first sermon
and will have nothing to preach next Sunday is half correct: the whole
gospel is crystallized in every sermon but next Sunday it will be
crystallized in a different form because the starting point is different
and the situation is different. If then a sermon is a crystallization, how
do we know if it is a faithful crystallization?

There is no automatic way of creating new crystallizations. It
might seem that if we took a passage of Scripture and made the
necessary situational and cultural changes, then we would have the
correct interpretation for ourselves. But what are the necessary and
correct cultural and situational alterations? This is precisely what is
at issue. Some of our situations are so different from those we encounter in Scripture that it is impossible for us, beginning with any given
situation in Scripture, to make such allowances and alterations that
we arrive at the situation with which we are concerned today. The
same is true of the change in culture. There is another and even
greater difficulty. The new crystallization is not the crystallization of
an isolated passage or a text; it must be a crystallization of what all
Scripture crystallizes in different ways. We cannot then simply free a
text of its cultural and situational limitations so that it speaks to us.
It is never the text which has to speak to us, but Christ whom the text
crystallizes. No trick of allegorization, universalization or identification in and of itself applied to a group of words in a passage or verse
will set Christ free, for there is the interplay between each text and
every other text, between the history of the church and every text, and
between the world today and every text. This can be put in another
way, again in keeping with the view of Scripture outlined earlier. We
do not read Paul's letters to discover the thoughts of Paul, not even
when suitably adapted to our situation, culture, and world-view; neither is it our aim to think Paul's thoughts after him, to think ourselves
into his skin and so express him today as we imagine he would have
expressed himself. We read Paul to reach the Christ whom Paul
experienced and experience him ourselves. It is not Paul or John or
Mark whom we seek to update and bring into our situation but Jesus
Christ.

How we do this will vary from passage to passage and subject to
subject. We have seen already[3] how even so remote a passage as

1 Peter 2:18–25, which deals with slavery, can yield in the light of the
rest of Scripture a basic view about man from which it is possible to
speak to those, including ourselves, who still depersonalize men
today. In a different kind of way when we ask why the exorcism stories
were included in the Gospel of Mark we discover that part of the
reason is the confession of the demons that Jesus is the Son of God
—even the most evil of creatures are seen to testify in some way to
Jesus. It might then be possible to search through the writings and
sayings of opponents of Christianity and find in them acknowledg-
ments of his greatness, if not his deity, and a sermon starting from an
exorcism account might end in listing modern testimonies to Jesus
from unexpected sources. Particular exorcism accounts can also be
used. Taking Luke 11:24–26, it remains true, even though we may not
believe in demons, that it is never sufficient to expel evil from a man's
life, or from society, and rest there; it must be replaced by good. If
a vacuum is left, evil will return, probably in a worse form. Only
positive good can ultimately displace wickedness. An entirely different method of crossing the bridge from the world of the Bible would
be applicable in a treatment of Luke 13:1–3, where Jesus is told about
some Galileans whose blood Pilate had mingled with their sacrifices,
with the implication that they must have been especially evil. Jesus
rejects the implication and warns his hearers that they also will perish
unless they repent. Contemporary Galilee was seething with nationalism and Jesus could see that if men did not turn away from it to God
then it would boil up into a terrible explosion in which the nation
would be destroyed by the Romans. The society in which we live is
probably not gripped by nationalism, but there are equally strong and
corrupting fevers which may control its members, e.g., the desire for
financial security which on the surface, like nationalism, seems a good
quality. A sermon using Luke 13:1–3 might not start with the passage
but with a concrete local illustration of someone who in a straightforward and honest way has sought to improve the position in society
of himself and his family but has ended in making an utter mess of
his life and theirs, and perhaps the lives also of others, because of the
very desire for security; the sermon would begin there and work
through the Lukan passage to a warning against the pervasive and
apparently good but really destructive spirit perverting society.

As these examples illustrate there is no simple technique by which we may make an easy transference from a biblical situation to our situation, but having framed what we believe to be a new crystallization, is there any way in which we can test it to see if it accords with the crystallization which we hold to be known in the New Testament? We might answer that it would be a satisfactory crystallization if it accorded with the facts of the New Testament. But what are the facts of the New Testament? We may say that our crystallization relates the death of Jesus to some situation in our life and culture. But the death of Jesus itself, while it may be a fact, is much more than a simple fact in the New Testament. As fact it always carries its own significance or interpretation; it is part of God's plan; it is his victory over Satan; it is the means by which sins are forgiven. Does then the way we interpret the death of Jesus in relation to our situation accord with the interpretation, or one of the interpretations, given in Scripture? But we are again in the position in which we have to make allowances for necessary cultural and situational changes, and this is the great difficulty. There is more than one interpretation of the significance of the death of Jesus in the New Testament. Even more importantly there is no reason to suppose that we are limited in our understanding of the death of Jesus to precisely those interpretations which exist in Scripture, nor even to those developed during the course of Christian history.

We might ask instead whether our crystallization accords with what we take in a general way to be the overall trend of Scripture. In the first chapter we saw how difficult it was to determine a central core of the significance that Scripture gives to Christ which actually says something precise about him. It may be, however, that we could take some inner principle derived from Scripture as its overall trend and use it as a yardstick with which to test our interpretations. Of course there is not even agreement as to what this overall trend is; different readers of Scripture intuit it in different ways. (a) Luther chose the doctrine of justification by faith. But: (i) As Luther realized there are parts of Scripture which do not accord with this principle; are we to leave them aside? (ii) Justification by faith is an essentially individualistic and personal doctrine; it may have been satisfactory in an age when life was lived in an individualistic way; but life is not lived like that now; many of our problems arise from this change, and it has always been difficult to express the doctrine of justification by faith as a social rather than an individualistic doctrine. (b) Liberal theology selected the teaching of Jesus as the true yardstick. But: (i) Few New Testament scholars today would have the confidence of the liberal theologians that the teaching of Jesus can be adequately unravelled. (ii) Jesus' teaching was culturally and situationally limited; he did not deal with many of the problems with which we are faced. (iii) Few would accept the simple distinction the liberals made between the Jesus of history and the Christ of the Church; the Christ of Christianity is at one and the same time both the historical Jesus and the preached Christ.

We may then be inclined to inquire if the crystallization which results from our interpretation accords with the existing general Christian world-view or with the existing Christian sub-culture. This is a valuable criterion, though difficult to apply accurately in practice. For in the first place there are legitimate variations within the existing Christian world-view arising from denominational and unsolved theological differences. Thus a crystallization which appears at home and valid within one particular denominational tradition, may appear very foreign in another. In the second place, the general pattern of the Christian world-view is itself continuously changing, and preachers, who are thinking people, ought to be assisting it to change. This means that our interpretations may at any given moment always be slightly different from the general pattern. Again the very fact of a gradually evolving culture and of changing situations in the world requires ever new understandings. It is often because men have argued that a particular understanding has not been in line with that which prevailed in their father's time that they have classed as heretical views which later have been seen to be real advances. If the thinking of a Luther or a Wesley had remained entirely within the existing Christian sub-culture they would never have enabled the Church to take the new steps to which they led it. Perhaps all we can say is that, given time, we must be able to convince others that our crystallization is a true crystallization. If we cannot do this then we should abandon it. This reference to others is important. The understanding of Scripture is never an individualistic activity. We belong within a Christian community and our thought in large part derives from it; this is true whether we think of a world-wide denomination or a house group. Our friends in both will help us to evolve our understanding. We have to learn to lean on them, to put our views to them, and to be ready to have them shot to pieces. Even if they are shot to pieces our understanding will have stimulated them and we ourselves will have been both stimulated in return and corrected.

At this point it might seem appropriate to ask about the function of exegesis. Have those who attended a theological seminary or a faculty of divinity completely wasted their time in their study of the New Testament? Exegesis has a real but negative function. It cannot tell us how to move from a text to the new crystallization, but if we are using a text or a passage, it can show us whether the interpretation which we have given is a legitimate understanding of the original passage. It can exclude false understanding, but it cannot in and of itself create new understanding. The new understanding arises from the encounter between the text and the situation and culture of today. In 1 Corinthians 1:22 Paul summarizes the attitude of the non-Christian world toward Christ using the traditional Jewish division of Jew and Greek/Gentile; in this way everyone is included. We would not attempt to include everyone in a similar categorization. In the ancient world with very few exceptions both Jew and Greek acknowledged the existence of the divine in some form or other; Jew and Greek stand for two attitudes towards the divine; the former waits for the divine to attest itself by some mighty deed; the latter represents those who attempt to seek it out for themselves. We in Western civilization would have to add a third category: those who are totally indifferent to God, who neither expect God to attest himself nor attempt to discover him for themselves. It would then be wrong to try to force everyone into the two categories of Jew or Greek; we must allow another category. So our culture forces us to describe the original comprehensiveness in a new way but that does not imply that Christ is no longer a stumbling-block or foolishness. The challenge to the preacher is the working out in detail of the additional category (there may be more than one additional category) and seeing how Christ stands in relation to it. This will help him in his approach to those who belong to this particular category, as well as leading him more fully into Paul's real meaning.

It is here that the academic exegete is left behind; he can see where

the exegesis points but he must leave it to those more involved in the
life of a congregation and in the society of nonbelievers to advance
along the new ways; all he can do is to see whether the interpreter's
understanding is on the right lines or not. It is because the function
of exegesis is negative that so much of what appeared in Chapter 3
was negative. If the exegete speaks positively he may be going outside
the area of his competence.

But equally there is no guarantee that if the interpretation passes
the exegete's scrutiny there will be a genuine crystallization. The
interpretation may be sound, but only sound! It is necessary, moreover, to recognize that the exegesis may be wholly wrong and the
Word be preached. A preacher may know what God has given him
to say to this congregation on this day in this situation and he may
say it even though he has started from a text of which it is not the
meaning; he may have used wrongly one of the verbal techniques
which we have been examining as a means for transforming the text
into a truth of God for his situation. That successful preaching takes
place in this way is no excuse for bad exegesis. Almost certainly the
sermon could have been preached on the basis of good exegesis, not
necessarily from a particular text, but from a mind alive to the whole
biblical spectrum and reflecting its use of the biblical material at
appropriate points throughout the sermon. Maybe it would have been
better for the preacher to have done without a formal text and just
proclaimed the Word God had given him.

(5) There is, then, no rule for creating new crystallizations. There
is no technique or skill which can be learned. It is possible to learn
how to put words together, how to present an argument in a convinc-
ing way, and how to capitalize upon that conviction so that it becomes
action, but all this deals only with what is superficial and not with the
understanding which is being presented. When we move from cultures
which are many millennia remote from us and into situations which
are very different from those that existed long ago, then we are carrying through a translation which is much greater than that from one
language into another. A parallel may be that of the fairy story
translated into ballet. The story remains; we recognize its main outline; we see its turning points; yet everything is different.

Because there is this act of translation which is almost a re-creation many modern freezings may appear to differ, indeed they will differ. When we examined the biblical freezings we saw that they differed; this arose partly from the failure of the biblical writers fully to express Jesus in their situation, partly because freezings in different situations and cultures would necessarily appear different and seemingly contradictory. The same will happen today. Our failures to express Jesus in our situation because of our own human weakness may be greater or less than those of the biblical writers but our situations are so very much more varied not just in comparison with theirs but in comparison with those of our fellow-Christians, and culture is so much less uniform, that we may expect that our understandings of what he means for us will look enormously different. We should realize that this is normal and not be alarmed by it.

It is valuable here to distinguish between the work of the craftsman and that of the technician. The technician has the skills he has been taught and which he applies again and again; he has a limited objective and provided he does not err in the use of his skills he will always achieve his objective, but the results are limited and predictable; there is a necessary repetitiveness about them. The craftsman may use the same skills but he is not just repeating a pattern; he moves out into new territory and achieves new results. The same man may be both. As a technician the photographer may take hundreds of passport photographs; he sets the subject down in the prescribed seat, turns on the lights, presses the button, develops and prints, and the result, if not very elegant, is always there. As a craftsman the photographer has from time to time to make a portrait; he picks a suitable chair, various accessories, alters the background, moves around the lights, experiments with angles, varies the development and printing, enlarges only a part of the negative; and the result is a portrait which exposes something of the subject's character. The glass-blower technician in the chemistry laboratory carries through hundreds of routine jobs and sometimes in his spare time creates a work of art. The preacher can never be the technician; he must always be the craftsman. There are no rules to be applied by which, given a text, the Word will be preached. The craftsman always knows he cannot do certain things; the techniques he has been taught should have made him aware of that; there are rules he must not break and we have examined some of them. If he knows what he cannot do, he never knows what he can. He must abide by the rules, use his skills and under God the Word will be heard. The craftsman photographer must keep to the technical rules; not stand between the lens and his subject, attend to the focusing of his camera, not shine all his lights into the lens. The craftsman preacher must keep to the rules: see his text in its context, not allegorize, not universalize what is limited to a particular situation. As he does this he must fear one thing above all: his own cleverness. A good sermon challenges to action; it does not leave its hearers admiring its artistry, its elegance, its cleverness or its charm.

Does this lay a terrible strain on the preacher? It does, but he is not without help. We have already seen the assistance that comes to us because we are members of the Christian community. It is just as essential that the preacher should remember the activity of the Spirit. He is said in John's Gospel (14:26; 15:26; 16:13) to lead Christians into an understanding of the truth. Paul says that there is a charisma, a spiritual gift, of the utterance of wisdom and knowledge (1 Cor. 12:8). When Paul makes judgments in actual situations sometimes he claims to have a word of the Lord to settle the matter, but at other times he gives his opinion as one who by the Lord's mercy is trustworthy (1 Cor. 7:10,25). So it is with the preacher; sometimes the word he needs can be taken easily from Scripture and related to his situations; at other times he can only speak as one who believes he has the mind of Christ (1 Cor. 2:16). In this confidence and only in it can he go forward to understand and to speak, and in this confidence he must go forward. It is not, however, true that this gift of understanding goes with academic knowledge. Many Christians, unlearned in a technical sense, offer an immediate, almost an instinctive, reaction to a new situation which we, who would like to exegete a little more deeply before we commit ourselves, realize is the true reaction; we perceive that in their reaction lies the mind of Christ.

(6) Finally and most importantly of all, the ultimate translation that we make whether as preachers or as those who meditate on Scripture for ourselves, is not from one set of words in Scripture into another set of words in a sermon or a discussion group, but from one

life into another life. Scripture is the crystallization of Christ within certain situations and cultures. Our sermons or our understandings are new crystallizations. But the real crystallization is the crystallization which takes place in our life or in the lives of those to whom we communicate our understanding. The result of our understanding will be either the re-creation of ourselves as individuals, or the re-creation of the Christian community, or even of the secular community. The ultimate test of our understanding is this re-creation. It is important to stress the church rather than the individual Christian; for it is the church which is the body of Christ. The purpose of all understanding of Scripture is to make Christ appear in his church so that he shapes that church to be like himself. The purpose of preaching is the formation of the church to be the true body of Christ. The purpose of the devotional study of Scripture is the harmonizing of the individual into the whole which is the church. But the preacher needs to remember that there are more factors at work than his preaching in the shaping of the church to be the true body of Christ. Certainly this takes place through worship and in the sacraments, but it also takes place as the individual members come to their own understanding, form in themselves a new crystallization, and so contribute to the upbuilding of the whole body. The movement is then from Christ through the crystallizations which are Scripture and the history of the church into the crystallization of the sermon and out again to be the life of the Church, which is the life of the risen Lord, and the only crystallization that really counts.

notes

Chapter 1

1. Edgar Hennecke and Wilhelm Schneemelcher, *New Testament Apocrypha,* Vol. I, ed. R. McL. Wilson (Lutterworth: London, 1963), pp. 146–147. Cf. Gospel of the Ebionites, *ibid.,* pp. 157–158, Gospel of the Hebrews, *ibid.,* pp. 163–164.
2. The parable of the Lost Sheep continued to be used in many different ways, especially by those outside the orthodox church; cf. Gospel of Thomas, *ibid.,* 107; Kendrick Grobel, *Gospel of Truth* (Nashville: Abingdon, 1960), 31.35—32.25; Irenaeus, *Against Heresies* I. 8,4; 16.1; II. 24.6.
3. For an instance of the value of James in the younger churches see Kosuke Koyama, *Waterbuffalo Theology* (SCM: London, 1974), pp. 161–9.
4. These are generalizations and the exceptions in each case are numerous.
5. Cf. Hans von Campenhausen, *The Formation of the Christian Bible,* (London: A. and C. Black Ltd, 1972), p. 105, "It is no accident that all the efforts to establish a fixed 'apostolic' confession of faith, or a definable 'primitive christian catechism', have come to grief. All the convergences and all the formal agreements which we possess alongside the variations and deviations only attest a certain toughness and trustworthiness in the tradition, but no more than that."

Chapter 2

1. See *5th Thule Expedition Report 1921–24,* 10 Vols. (Nordisk Forlag: Copenhagen, various dates).
2. It is, perhaps, difficult for those who belong to urban culture to see how an animal may be intensely cared for and then used for food but the following quotation from *The Listener* (London: British Broadcasting Corporation) of 14th August, 1975, p. 204, from a radio talk by Don Haworth, may help us: "The weeds were served with home-baked bread

made from their own grain and a piece of pork that had once been part of John's close friend. 'There's very little room for sentiment on a farm,' he said, 'particularly one of this size, where every single inch of ground and every animal has to pay its way. The last pig I killed, we shared half with a neighbour and the other half is salted and hanging in the outhouse. I took him to the slaughterhouse, and I waited half an hour or so with him in the waiting chamber.'

" 'John very much likes fat bacon,' Shirley said, 'and he's rather good about this thing of do I, or don't I [sic], eat my own animal. Before he came here, he had a pig almost as a pet. It followed him around like a dog, and went for walks and so on. Then time came for it to be killed. He had it hanging up in the cellar, and he solemnly ate his way through it for three years. And then he went vegetarian, simply because he couldn't face bought meat after that. There was just nothing that would measure up to the beauty of this particular experience, eating the pig to whom he'd given his love and care, and then she'd given back her meat, which was her way of returning his love.' " (Permission granted to reprint.)

3. Pp. 65 ff.
4. "My great, dead friend, Leo Szilard, wrote to me the most beautiful sentence about biology. He said: 'What we physicists brought into biology was the conviction that anything that exists in nature man can understand.' " J. Bronowski, *The Listener,* 3rd July, 1975, p. 12.
5. Pp. 62 ff.
6. This is an exaggeration; the ancients practiced irrigation and so made some attempt to manipulate nature.
7. J.R. Ravetz, *Scientific Knowledge and Its Social Problems,* (London: Penguin Books, 1973), p. 12.
8. See R. Gill, *The Social Context of Theology,* (London: Mowbrays, 1975), p. 58.
9. Returned missionaries have told me how much more difficult they have found it to preach the gospel in industrial Glasgow than in some of the less advanced areas of the world.
10. Cf. R.H.S. Boyd, *India and the Latin Captivity of the Church: The Cultural Context of the Gospel* (London: Cambridge University Press, 1974); J.A. Veitch, "Is an Asian Theology Possible?" *Scottish Journal of Theology* 28 (1975), 27–43.
11. See Werner Georg Kümmel, *The New Testament: The History of the Investigation of Its Problems,* (London: SCM, 1973).

Chapter 3

1. See above p. 41.
2. See below pp. 65 ff.

3. In the first draft of this manuscript my secretary misheard the word "goal" and typed it as "God." It is a fair criticism of much of my work and that of my colleagues!

4. Origen, *Commentary on John,* 10:16. (Translation as in *The Ante-Nicene Fathers* Vol. X (Grand Rapids, Mich.: Eerdmans, 1951).

5. *Ibid.* 10:18.

6. *Fables of Aesop,* trans., S.A. Handford (London: Penguin Classics, 1954), p. 12.

7. Origen, *Commentary on Matthew,* 11:3 (translation as note 4 above).

8. Cf. W. Wink, *The Bible in Human Transformation,* (Philadelphia: Fortress Press, 1973), pp. 49ff.

9. *Discerning the Signs of the Times,* (London: SCM, 1946), pp. 26–39.

10. Cf. p. 35 where we saw that what Paul had to say is very relevant in other parts of the world. This is true of much that he writes.

11. See my article, "The Interpretation of Tongues," *Scottish Journal of Theology* 28 (1975), 45–62.

12. Col. 3:18–4:1; Eph. 5:22–6:9; 1 Pet. 2:13–3:7.

13. I have never heard a Protestant preacher apply Isaiah 43:6, "I will say to the north, Give up," to the situation in Northern Ireland!

14. See n. 11.

15. Translation from Hennecke and Schneemelcher (ed. Wilson), *op. cit.,* pp. 517–518.

16. J.H. Newman, *Parochial and Plain Sermons,* (London: Rivingtons 1873), Vol. I, pp. 57ff.

17. We have the same difficulty in understanding "sacrifice"; it is not a feature of our society.

18. The sayings of the Sermon on the Mount are not in their original setting but in a new setting.

19. *Sermons,* Second Series (London: Kegan Paul, Trench, Trübner, 1898), pp. 1ff.

20. Harry Emerson Fosdick, *A Great Time to Be Alive,* (London: SCM, 1945), pp. 21–30.

21. *Op. cit.,* pp. 27ff.

22. Cf. Wink, *op. cit.* We need to "resonate" (Wink's word) with the character in the story and find the "paralytic" or "scribe" in ourselves.

23. Arthur John Gossip, *From the Edge of the Crowd,* (Edinburgh: T. & T. Clark, 1924), pp. 68–69.

Chapter 4

1. See above pp. 18 ff.

2. A more detailed treatment of this issue will be found in my *A Commen-*

tary on the First and Second Epistles to the Thessalonians in Harper's New Testament Commentaries, ed., Henry Chadwick (New York: Harper & Row, 1972), pp. 359ff.
3. See above p. 69 f.

DATE DUE

DEC 1 3 2002			